YOUNG WOMEN MUTUAL ACTIVITIES

Other Titles By The Authors:

Dating For Under A Dollar: 301 Ideas

The Dance Book:
555 Ways to Ask, Answer, and Plan For Dances

The Book of Mormon Vocabulary Guide

The Doctrine & Covenants Vocabulary Guide

Young Men Mutual Activities

This book is not an officical publication
of The Church of Jesus Christ of Latter-day Saints
nor is it endorsed by the Church.

Printed in the United States of America

YOUNG WOMEN MUTUAL ACTIVITIES

Blair & Tristan Tolman

For
Tanner, Shaundi, Brennan, and Jaxon
with love

CONTENTS

Introduction

Frequently, young women of The Church of Jesus Christ of Latter-day Saints and their youth leaders meet together to plan mutual activities for the upcoming weeks. Sometimes, these brainstorming and planning meetings turn into blank stares and "brain drizzles." Our purpose in writing this book is to help keep mutual activity ideas flowing for both youth and their leaders in such situations. Use the ideas found in this book to plan fun, meaningful mutual activities of many kinds.

Since every activity should be planned with a meaningful purpose in mind, this book provides hundreds of "purposeful" ideas meant to help young women learn, understand, and incorporate the seven Young Women Values into their lives by focusing on them in their weekly mutual activities. We have attempted to provide a wide variety of ideas in each chapter, some of which can be used for regular weekly mutual activities, some for larger-scale activities such as New Beginnings, Standards Night, and Young Women in Excellence, and some for monthly combined activities with the young men. Although the chapters in this book divide the activity ideas according to which value each activity teaches, the seven Young Women Values are so intertwined that often, a single activity naturally reinforces more than one value at a time. Where this is the case, we have categorized that activity into the chapter of one of the values it reinforces, though it may also reinforce others.

Often, as young women participate in mutual activities, they fulfill Personal Progress requirements without even knowing it. This book identifies many mutual activities which may help girls complete Personal Progress Value Experiences, thus encouraging young women and their leaders to plan activities which are not only fun and purposeful, but which also help the girls advance in the Personal Progress Program as well. This is not meant to be a comprehensive list of activities that fulfill Value Experiences, but only a compilation of several possible applications that may help girls fulfil these experiences.

It is our hope that as you use this book to plan mutual activities with a purpose, you will help the young women better understand and love the Young Women Values, work towards earning their Young Womanhood Recognition Awards, and enjoy playing, learning, and growing with each other every week at mutual.

chapter one

Faith

Ancestor Scrapbooks

Make ancestor scrapbooks together. Design pages to put in the scrapbooks with spaces where the girls can fill in information about the ancestors' names, lives, and families. Either have the girls come prepared with information about their ancestors that they can include in their books, or prepare the pages at mutual and let the girls fill in the pages with information after they get home. Provide craft scissors, colored paper, and decorative materials for the girls to use to make their scrapbooks attractive and unique.

** Helps fulfill a Mia Maid 1 Individual Worth Value Experience and a Mia Maid 2 Individual Worth Value Experience*

Variation: Make ancestor photo albums. With their parents' permission, have the girls bring as many different photographs of their ancestors as possible to this activity. Using care to handle the photographs properly, let the girls arrange the photographs on picture pedigree charts, in photo albums, or in frames for the girls' families to view and enjoy.

** Helps fulfill a Mia Maid 1 Individual Worth Value Experience and a Mia Maid 2 Individual Worth Value Experience and may help fulfill a Beehive 1 Individual Worth Value Experience*

"And Thus We See. . ."

The young women should bring their scriptures to this activity. Search through the scriptures for verses that contain the phrase, "And thus we see. . ." This phrase should alert them that an important message or lesson in the scriptures is about to be given. The girls should highlight the lesson that follows each "and thus we see" phrase as well as make a list of those lessons on paper. Then, discuss the list they have compiled. Ask the girls, "Why do you think the scriptures taught that lesson or included that message?" Let the young women apply these teachings to their own lives.

Blind Date

As a mutual activity for the Laurels, the class advisor should set up a blind date for the Laurels to meet new LDS guys. The advisor can bring her husband to this activity! Make sure that the activity allows for plenty of interaction and communication, suitable for a first date for teenagers. The Laurels should plan as much of this date as possible, while receiving guidance and suggestions from their leaders.

Book of Mormon: Another Testament of Jesus Christ

Look up "Jesus Christ" in the Topical Guide of your scriptures and make a list of the names and titles by which the Savior is known. Then, search the *Book of Mormon* as a class, looking for pages that do not contain a reference to the Savior somewhere on the page. Count the number of pages that do not mention Him in some way. This activity will illustrate how frequently the *Book of Mormon* does in fact testify of the Savior, and will reaffirm to the girls that the *Book of Mormon* is truly "Another Testament of Jesus Christ."

Book of Mormon Read-In

Have all the girls bring beanbag chairs and their personal copies of the *Book of Mormon.* Sit in a room together and read the *Book of Mormon* for the entire mutual activity. You could take turns reading out loud together or read silently on your own.

Book of Mormon Testimonies

Obtain several copies of the *Book of Mormon* from either your ward mission leader or the full-time missionaries in your area. Carefully glue typed copies of your class members' testimonies in the front of each book, and include a photograph of your class if you desire. With the mission leader's permission, highlight important verses such as Moroni 10:3-5 with a red colored pencil. Then, either distribute the books to your nonmember friends or return them to your ward mission leader or the full-time missionaries for distribution.

** Helps fulfill a Beehive 2 Faith Value Experience and a Mia Maid 2 Faith Value Experience*

Book Review

Prior to this activity, each girl must obtain a copy of the book *The Miracle of Forgiveness* by President Spencer W. Kimball (or another book approved by the Young Women leader) and read it on her own. For the activity, have a book review on this book. Each girl brings her copy. Discuss things that the young women learned from the book and everyone's favorite parts of it.

** May help fulfill a Mia Maid 2 Knowledge Value Experience*

Campfire Stories

Sit around a campfire and tell uplifting stories to each other. Good campfire stories might come from pioneer journals, personal journals, or Church magazines. As a treat, make S'mores over the fire by roasting large marshmallows and putting one marshmallow with a few squares of chocolate in between two graham crackers. You could also heat water over your campfire and make hot chocolate to sip during the stories, if you desire.

Canning

Exercise faith in the prophet's counsel to store food by canning fruits or vegetables as a class. If your young women don't have produce from their own gardens to preserve, offer to help ward members who do. Suggest that they provide the supplies and your class provide the labor.

** May help fulfill a Beehive 1 Good Works Value Experience, a Beehive 2 Good Works Value Experience, a Mia Maid 1 Knowledge Value Experience, a Mia Maid 1 Good Works Value Experience, a Mia Maid 2 Knowledge Value Experience, and a Mia Maid 2 Good Works Value Experience*

Cemetery Hunting

Go to a local cemetery. Search for the headstones of deceased relatives and check the headstone information for accuracy against your genealogical records. Let the girls photograph the headstones of their relatives for documentation purposes. While at their headstones, read journal articles or other stories from the lives of those relatives.

Variation: While you are at the cemetery, perform a service project to beautify the area. Stand flowers back up in their pots, sweep dirt and leaves off the headstones, and remove any grass that has grown over and covered the words on the headstones.

Church Videos

Check out a few Church videos from your ward library. Bring blankets and pillows, get comfortable, and watch Church videos together. If the videos are short, consider watching Church commercials ("The Homefront Series") in between the videos.

Conversion Stories

Invite ward or stake members who are recent converts to the Church to come and share their conversion stories with the young women. Ask them to talk about the role and importance of the full-time missionaries and the Church members in their conversions, and to testify of the conversion power of the *Book of Mormon.*

** Helps fulfill a Beehive 1 Faith Value Experience*

Family Proclamation Study

Make a copy of *The Family: A Proclamation To The World,* a proclamation given by the First Presidency and Council of the Twelve Apostles of the Church, for each young woman in your class. Each young woman should bring a package of colored pencils or a box of crayons to this activity. Sit around a table together and review and discuss the proclamation in depth. Encourage the girls to highlight those sections of the proclamation that reinforce any one of the seven Young Women Values. Encourage the girls to underline these sections with the appropriate value colors using their crayons or colored pencils. Then in the margins of the proclamation, write phrases of the Young Women Theme that resemble the message of the proclamation.

Variation: Let the girls select a variety of topics discussed in the proclamation and write these in a vertical column on a chalkboard (for example: marriage, love, children, and parental responsibility). Next to these topics, write statements explaining what the world believes about these topics. Then, read the proclamation together to find out what the First Presidency and Council of the Twelve Apostles believe and counsel regarding these topics. Discuss with your girls the differences between the world's view and the Lord's view, and how important it is to listen to and follow the Prophet of the Church.

Fireside

Have a fireside around a real fire, outside. Have a good youth speaker come. Roast marshmallows for refreshments, or make S'mores over the fire by roasting large marshmallows and putting one marshmallow with a few squares of chocolate in between two graham crackers. If the weather is too cold to host this activity outdoors, hold the fireside inside a ward member's home around a fireplace.

** May help fulfill a Mia Maid 2 Knowledge Value Experience*

Variation: Ask at least two converts to the Church to come and speak at the fireside. Have them tell your group about their conversions to the Gospel. Prepare the girls beforehand to ask questions of the converts such as, "How did you gain your testimony?" "How

did your family feel about your decision to join the Church?" "What is your favorite teaching of the Church?"
** Helps fulfill a Beehive 1 Faith Value Experience and may help fulfill a Mia Maid 2 Knowledge Value Experience*

Variation: Have a "morningside" instead. Find a comfortable place to meet before school or on a Saturday morning, bring in a good youth speaker, and let the speaker give a talk. Follow with a testimony meeting and, if time permits, eat breakfast together after the morningside is over.
** May help fulfill a Mia Maid 2 Knowledge Value Experience*

Gospel Questions

A week or two prior to this activity, ask each girl to write on slips of paper several Gospel questions she would like answered. Give these questions to a member of the bishopric and ask him to study them prayerfully and come to your mutual activity prepared to answer the questions and hold a Gospel-centered discussion about them.

Hymn Study

Provide a *Hymns* book for each class member. Let each young woman select at least one hymn to study as a class. For each hymn, do the following: read the words of each hymn out loud and talk about its meaning. Then, look up the scriptures referenced at the bottom of the hymn and read the verses aloud. Consider how those scriptures apply to the hymn and talk about any new understanding about the hymn gained from reading those verses. After studying and discussing it, sing the hymn together as a class.
** Helps fulfill a Beehive 1 Knowledge Value Experience and may help fulfill a Mia Maid 1 Faith Value Experience, a Mia Maid 1*

Knowledge Value Experience, and a Mia Maid 2 Choice And Accountability Value Experience

Institute Update

Ask the LDS Church Educational System Institute teacher in your area to come and speak to your girls (especially Laurels) about the benefits of attending Institute after they graduate from high school. Request that he give the girls specific information about class times, requirements, and topics. Discuss the Institute program of the Church as it applies to college students as well as non-college students, and list the class options which are available for both types of young adults. To help your girls feel more comfortable with the transition to college and Institute life, this mutual activity could be held at the Institute building.

Journal Writing

Host a journal writing workshop. Let each girl bring her journal to mutual and share some ideas and writing techniques that work for her. Talk about what kinds of things would be especially valuable to record in a journal. If possible, ask a mature adult who kept a journal during her teenage years to come to this activity and talk about what types of things she is glad she recorded, and what she wishes she would have recorded during her life as a young woman. Then, spend part of the activity actually writing in your journals.

** May help fulfill a Beehive 1 Choice And Accountability Value Experience, a Beehive 2 Individual Worth Value Experience, a Mia Maid 1 Faith Value Experience, a Mia Maid 2 Faith Value Experience, a Mia Maid 2 Individual Worth Value Experience, and a Mia Maid 2 Choice And Accountability Value Experience*

Member Missionary Work

Ask the full-time missionaries in your area or some returned missionaries to come and speak to your group about ways that you can become more involved in missionary work. Talk about the importance of being member missionaries and give specific ways your class can serve as missionaries in your homes, at school, and in your community.

** Helps fulfill a Beehive 1 Faith Value Experience and a Mia Maid 2 Faith Value Experience*

Missionary Discussions

As a class, read and become familiar with the Church missionary discussions. Then, divide the girls into pairs and ask them to practice teaching principles of the first discussion to the other members of the group.

** Helps fulfill a Mia Maid 2 Faith Value Experience*

Missionary Journal Reading

Invite any or all of the members of the bishopric of your ward to this activity, and ask them to bring their missionary journals with them. Take turns asking the girls their birthdays and letting the bishopric members turn to those dates in their mission journals and read the entries aloud. (Censorship at the discretion of the bishopric members is obviously allowed.)

Missionary Presentations

Invite three or four returned missionaries from different missions to give 15 minute presentations on their missions, with a few minutes at the end of each one for the youth to ask questions.

Parable Writing

For this activity, give each girl a piece of paper and a pencil and ask her to write her own parable. To begin, teach the girls what parables are and look at examples of parables in the scriptures. Then, each girl must come up with a principle she wants to teach and then write a story which indirectly teaches the principle by telling a story. When all the girls have written their parables, let them read them to each other and let the other girls guess what principles they are trying to teach. For additional challenge, require the girls to write their parables in scriptural language, using appropriate scriptural words such as "ye," "thee," and "thus."

Priesthood Appreciation

Study and learn about the offices, organization, and duties of the Aaronic and Melchizedek Priesthoods. If possible, invite some priesthood holders to your class (possibly worthy young men) to talk about the priesthood and to answer questions. Focus also on specific things the girls can do to respect the priesthood and to sustain their priesthood leaders.

** Helps fulfill a Mia Maid 1 Choice And Accountability Value Experience*

Record Extraction

Invite the ward or stake name extraction specialist to teach your young women about the record extraction program of the Church. Let the young women practice entering name extraction data into a computer and get firsthand experience with this skill. If appropriate, invite each girl to participate in the record extraction program on a long-term basis by completing at least one packet on her own time (packets can be obtained from the record extraction specialist in your area).

** Helps fulfill a Mia Maid 1 Knowledge Value Experience*

Rejoice In Christ

Celebrate the life and teachings of the Savior by spending a mutual evening learning about Him. Give specific topics to the girls in your class such as "His premortal life," "His earth life," "His mission," "His resurrection," and "His atonement." Let the girls research in the scriptures to find as much information as possible about their assigned topics. Then take turns sharing what you have learned with the other girls in your class. Select several qualities that you admire about the Savior, and talk about ways that your group can help each other to develop those qualities in yourselves as you strive to become more like Him.

** Helps fulfill a Beehive 1 Divine Nature Value Experience and a Mia Maid 2 Divine Nature Value Experience*

Sacrament Cloths

With the permission of your priesthood leaders, wash and iron the cloths used at the sacrament table. Discuss the sacredness and the symbolism of the sacrament. Invite a worthy priest, teacher, and deacon to come to this activity and discuss their feelings about the sacrament and administering it. Have each of these young men tell about his specific duties in administering the sacrament.

** Helps fulfill a Beehive 1 Faith Value Experience and a Mia Maid 1 Good Works Value Experience and may help fulfill a Beehive 2 Good Works Value Experience, a Mia Maid 2 Faith Value Experience, and a Mia Maid 2 Good Works Value Experience*

Variation: Wash and iron stake baptismal clothing or kitchen drying towels and hot pads.

** Helps fulfill a Mia Maid 1 Good Works Value Experience*

Satellite Broadcast

Obtain from your ward or stake library a videotape of a satellite broadcast produced by the Church and watch it together for mutual. After the broadcast, discuss what you have learned. To help the girls focus on the broadcast better, consider previewing the broadcast before mutual and making up a quiz using information from the broadcast. Have the young women answer the questions as they watch the broadcast.

** Helps fulfill a Mia Maid 2 Knowledge Value Experience*

Scripture Search

Search the scriptures for information about specific topics to see what the scriptures say about various problems and challenges of the latter days. Teach the young women how to use the Topical Guide, the Bible Dictionary, the Index, and footnotes in their searches. Some topics you might search for: government, signs of the times, obedience, love, service, agency, good works, being peacemakers, or repentance.

** May help fulfill a Beehive 1 Faith Value Experience, a Beehive 1 Choice And Accountability Value Experience, a Mia Maid 1 Divine Nature Value Experience, a Mia Maid 1 Choice And Accountability Value Experience, a Mia Maid 2 Faith Value Experience, a Mia Maid 2 Choice And Accountability Value Experience, and a Mia Maid 2 Good Works Value Experience*

Scripture Skits

Divide your girls into small groups and assign each

group a scripture story to read, rehearse, and act out in play format. If you desire, let the girls make simple props to use in their skits before they perform for each other.

**May help fulfill a Mia Maid 1 Individual Worth Value Experience, a Mia Maid 1 Good Works Value Experience, a Mia Maid 1 Integrity Value Experience, and a Mia Maid 2 Knowledge Value Experience*

Temple Dress Bags

As a class, sew white temple dress bags for the girls to keep and use in the future to contain their temple clothes. A good pattern for temple dress bags can be found in *Creative Homemaking For Happy Living: Relief Society Homemaking Booklet* (The Church of Jesus Christ of Latter Day Saints, 1984, pp.107-108).

**May help fulfill a Mia Maid 1 Knowledge Value Experience and a Mia Maid 2 Knowledge Value Experience*

Variation: As a class, sew white, satin-covered hangers for the girls to keep and use in the future to hang up their temple wedding dresses.

**May help fulfill a Mia Maid 1 Knowledge Value Experience and a Mia Maid 2 Knowledge Value Experience*

Temple Recommend Preparation

Ask a member of the bishopric to speak to the girls about temple recommends. Focus on the requirements needed to obtain one and the value of having one (or until they are old enough, the value of living worthy of one). This activity is especially appropriate shortly before a youth temple trip.

Value Books

This activity should be held in your ward library. Let the

girls go through several Church magazines located in your ward library such as the *Ensign,* the *New Era,* and the *Friend,* looking for articles that discuss one of the seven Young Women Values. They should bookmark these articles. When your group has selected several articles for each value, photocopy the articles (one copy for each young woman) and assemble them into Value Books for the girls to take home, read, and use as a resource.

**May help fulfill a Mia Maid 2 Knowledge Value Experience and a Mia Maid 2 Choice And Accountability Value Experience*

chapter two

Divine Nature

Bread For Sacrament Service

Learn to make homemade bread, and let each young woman take a loaf home. Donate a few loaves to the ward priesthood leaders to be used for the sacrament on the following Sunday.

** May help fulfill a Beehive 2 Good Works Value Experience, a Mia Maid 1 Knowledge Value Experience, a Mia Maid 1 Good Works Value Experience, a Mia Maid 2 Knowledge Value Experience, and a Mia Maid 2 Good Works Value Experience*

Church Callings

Invite at least three mature women in your ward who hold Church callings to come and speak to your girls about their callings. Ask them to discuss some of the specific assignments involved with their callings, their positive feelings about their callings, and the blessings that have come to them from giving Church service.

** Helps fulfill a Mia Maid 1 Good Works Value Experience*

Variation: With permission of your bishop, make

several handouts containing the following message by Elder Neal A. Maxwell, "God does not begin by asking about our ability, but only about our availability, and if we prove our dependability, He will increase our capability." Give the handouts to the bishop and his counselors to give away when they extend Church callings to ward members.

** May help fulfill a Beehive 1 Good Works Value Experience, a Beehive 2 Good Works Value Experience, and a Mia Maid 1 Good Works Value Experience*

Communication Connection

Invite the mothers of your young women to attend this activity with their daughters. Request that the mothers come dressed up like their daughters and the girls come dressed up like the mothers. Play "The Communication Connection," which is a game that asks mothers and daughters trivia questions about each other (questions written by you beforehand) to see how well they know each other.

Cross Stitch

Obtain or make a cross stitch pattern of a wall hanging with the words "I Am A Child of God" or that illustrates one or more of the Young Women Values. Provide supplies for each girl to cross stitch her own wall hanging, and cross stitch them together.

** Helps fulfill a Mia Maid 1 Integrity Value Experience and may help fulfill a Beehive 2 Good Works Value Experience, a Mia Maid 1 Knowledge Value Experience, and a Mia Maid 2 Knowledge Value Experience*

Daddy Daughter Date

Invite the dads of the girls to this activity. Have the girls' fathers come as their daughters' dates, and provide activities where the dads and the daughters work as teams and strengthen their relationships during the evening. If you desire, request the dads and daughters to come dressed in costumes of famous pairs (i.e. Beauty and the Beast or a king and a queen). You could also have a daddy daughter dance and teach dance steps from both eras, letting the dads and daughters dance as partners.

Families Forever

Invite speakers to visit your young women and discuss the importance and roles of the family. Some possible topics relating to the family are: The Family: A Proclamation to the World; Family Past; Family Present; Family Future; Family Home Evening; Family Fun; Family Roles; Families Forever.

Family History Center Visit

Visit a family history center in your area. Learn ways to find information about your ancestors. Practice using the computers, the microfilm readers, and the microfiche readers. Discuss the importance of family history work in the Church, and how your understanding of and appreciation for your family will grow as you do your genealogy.

**May help fulfill a Mia Maid 2 Individual Worth Value Experience*

Variation: While at the family history center, learn how to submit family names to a temple so that temple ordinances can be performed in behalf of deceased family members. Encourage the girls to each submit at least one of their ancestors' names to the temple, so that temple work can be performed for that person.

** Helps fulfill a Mia Maid 2 Individual Worth Value Experience*

Graduation Books

Shortly before seminary graduation or high school graduation, the young women leaders should contact several significant adults in the lives of the graduating Laurels and ask them to write letters to the Laurels stating their love for them, any special experiences shared with them, qualities about the girls which they admire, and their testimonies. The leaders should collect these letters and assemble them into books, one for each Laurel. Then, for mutual, have a graduation party for the girls and present the books to them as part of the activity.

Homemaking: A Full-Time Job

Have several respected women from the ward or stake who are full-time homemakers come to this activity to answer the young women's often answered question, "What does a homemaker do all day?" Also, ask those women who are mothers to discuss what they enjoy about being mothers and what advice they would give teenage girls about preparing for motherhood.

** Helps fulfill a Mia Maid 1 Divine Nature Value Experience*

Honor Thy Parents Night

Plan a class program to honor class members' parents. Invite the girls' families to attend the performance. Show pictures or slides of the parents when they were younger, play music from the parents' eras, tell how the parents met and/or got engaged, talk about the parents' hobbies, and end by letting the girls publicly tell their parents how much they love them.

"I Am A Child Of God"

Host an evening focusing on the girls' divine nature and divine parentage. Use the primary song "I Am A Child Of God" as your theme and invite speakers to come and talk to the girls about their Heavenly Father and their relationship to Him. Give each young woman an opportunity to finish this sentence, "I know that I am a child of God because . . ." as part of this presentation.

Letters To Mothers

As a group, write letters to your mothers. Have each girl express her love for her mother in the letter and write several specific things she admires about her. Design pretty stationery on which to write the letters, and enclose the letters in pretty envelopes that you have designed as well. Either stamp and mail the letters or let the girls take the letters home and hide them under their mothers' pillows for the mothers to discover.

** Helps fulfill a Beehive 1 Divine Nature Value Experience and a Beehive 1 Individual Worth Value Experience and may help fulfill a Mia Maid 1 Individual Worth Value Experience*

Variation: Write similar letters to the girls' fathers instead of to their mothers.

** Helps fulfill a Beehive 1 Divine Nature Value Experience and a Beehive 1 Individual Worth Value Experience and may help fulfill a Mia Maid 1 Individual Worth Value Experience*

Variation: Have the girls write letters to themselves. As a group, make pretty stationery and then write letters to themselves, stating their future goals, dreams, and plans. They should be as specific as they desire. When everyone has written their letters, seal them up in envelopes to be opened individually by the girls on their 18th birthdays.

** Helps fulfill a Mia Maid 2 Divine Nature Value Experience*

Marriage Blessings

Ask a married couple who has been married for many years and sealed in the temple to come and speak to your girls about the importance of temple marriage and the blessings of being sealed for time and eternity. Let the girls ask questions of the couple at the end of the presentation.

** Helps fulfill a Mia Maid 1 Divine Nature Value Experience and a Mia Maid 2 Divine Nature Value Experience*

Mormonads

For this mutual activity, combine your creative abilities and try to come up with new Mormonad poster ideas for the *New Era* magazine. A Mormonad is a poster that teaches a Gospel principle by using a catchy phrase and a visual image that reinforces the phrase. Begin by showing the young women several examples of Mormonads; after viewing them, come up with your own. Submit your ideas to the *New Era* for possible publication.

Mystery Mothers

Invite several mothers of young women to come to this activity and let the girls guess who they are. All mystery mothers should sit behind a partition, completely hidden from view. Assign each mystery mother a number by which she will be known until the end of the activity when her identity is revealed. Give each young woman a piece of paper and a pencil. To play, let the girls take turns asking questions to the mothers in an attempt to figure out their identities. For example, a young woman could ask, "Mother #2, what is your favorite flavor of ice cream?" or, "Mother #6, how did you meet your husband?" The mothers must answer their questions truthfully, but can disguise their voices if they choose. The girls should number their paper and write the guessed name of each mother next to her number. When the girls either think they know who the mothers are, or are totally baffled and out of questions, reveal the mothers and see how many of them the girls identified correctly.

Nature Walk

Take a field trip through a forest, grassland, or desert and identify the types of plants you find using plant identification books. Keep a list of the types of trees, shrubs, flowers, grasses, and algae you find there. Recognize and discuss the hand of Heavenly Father in the creation of the earth.

Recipe Book

Prepare for the divine role of motherhood by collecting favorite recipes from ward members and compiling them into a recipe book. Divide the book into sections such as appetizers, salads, breads, main dishes, desserts, and beverages. Make a copy of the book for each girl in your class. You might also make the recipe books available to other ward members. Be sure to credit each recipe to its contributor by listing the contributor's name next to the recipe.

**May help fulfill a Mia Maid 1 Knowledge Value Experience and a Mia Maid 2 Knowledge Value Experience*

Sew Crazy

Prepare for the divine role of motherhood by learning to sew any of the following items: a crocheted baby blanket, crocheted baby booties, a baby bunting, or an apron.

** May help fulfill a Beehive 2 Good Works Value Experience, a Mia Maid 1 Knowledge Value Experience, and a Mia Maid 2 Knowledge Value Experience*

Temple Concentration

As a class, make a Temple Concentration game to play together. Obtain or draw two small pictures of each Church temple and mount them on index cards. To play, turn all of the cards face down on a table and let one person begin by turning two cards face up, hoping to get a match. If that player gets matching pictures, she puts the match in her pile and goes again. If she does not get a match, the next player takes her turn. Play until all cards have been paired.

Variation: To make this game more challenging, require that whenever a player gets a match, she must properly identify the temple in order to keep the match. If she cannot give the correct name for the temple, she returns the cards to the table face down and play passes to the next player.

Temple Trivia

As a class, make a Temple Trivia game to play together. First, let the girls search through several Church magazines for interesting facts about temples such as when certain temples were constructed, which temples display statues of the angel Moroni, and which temples have been rededicated. Then, on several 3x5 index cards, write the trivia questions on one side and the answers on the other. To play, take turns choosing a trivia card, reading the question, and trying to answer it either individually or as a group.

> **Variation:** Play Apostle Trivia. Rather than searching for facts about temples, search for interesting facts about the lives of modern-day Apostles and write them as questions on index cards, with answers on the backs of the cards. You could include facts about their childhood experiences, professions, and families. Game rules are the same as for Temple Trivia.

You: The Prism of The Lord

For this activity, focus on the individual beauty of each young woman as she reflects the light of Christ in her everyday living. Use prisms and rainbows to decorate for this activity, which should remind the girls that as a crystal prism reflects many beautiful colors, they also, as daughters of God, reflect unique beauty and loveliness. For additional ideas along this theme, see Philippians 2:15, Proverbs 20:27, *Doctrine & Covenants* 11:13, and 3 Nephi 18:24.

You: The Youth of The Noble Birthright

This activity emphasizes the individual worth of your young women as youth of the latter days. Focus on the talk given by President Ezra Taft Benson on this subject (see *Ensign,* May 1986, pp.43-46) and what the girls must do to carry out their responsibilities on earth. Sing the Hymn "Carry On" as part of this activity (*Hymns* #255) and possibly even use portions of the soundtrack to the musical "Saturday's Warrior."

chapter three

Individual Worth

Access Ramp

As a class, build a wheelchair access ramp at a building in your community that does not currently provide wheelchair access into the premises. Talk to your girls about how important it is that businesses and people in your community be sensitive to the special needs of individuals in wheelchairs, and how you can make a positive difference for those individuals in your community.

** Helps fulfill a Beehive 1 Knowledge Value Experience, a Beehive 2 Knowledge Value Experience, a Beehive 2 Good Works Value Experience, a Mia Maid 1 Knowledge Value Experience, a Mia Maid 1 Good Works Value Experience, and a Mia Maid 2 Good Works Value Experience*

Be Your Own Kind of Beautiful

Write a skit or play together which emphasizes the importance of the individual, that young women don't have to try to be like someone else, but they can and should be their own kind of beautiful. Assign parts, rehearse, and act out your skit for the other young women, for the young men, or for the girls' parents. You might display the Mormonad entitled, "Be Your Own Kind of Beautiful" at this activity.

**May help fulfill a Mia Maid 1 Individual Worth Value Experience and a Mia Maid 2 Knowledge Value Experience*

Beauty Night

Plan an evening at your home when a beauty consultant can come, free of charge, to consult with each of the girls on their choices of makeup, hair care, nail care, and skin care. The consultant should bring several products for the girls to experiment with, and should guide the girls as to how to properly use the products and which ones work best for each individual girl. Make sure the consultant does not attempt to sell products to the girls at this activity.

Breakfast Surprise

As a welcome for new class members, have a surprise breakfast at a class member's or leader's home. Early on a Saturday morning with the girls' parents' approval, drive to class members' homes and wake them up out of bed. Kidnap them in their pajamas and take them to the home where breakfast will be served.

Variation: Plan a whole morning of activity to follow the breakfast. Include team building activities and/or service projects to help unite your class.

Christmas Ornaments for Church

Make Christmas ornaments that represent the Young Women program of the Church and use them to decorate an artificial Christmas tree for your ward meetinghouse. (You might need to locate and donate an artificial tree to your ward first, if it doesn't own one already.) Some ideas: a paper chain made from colored construction paper (use the seven Young Women value colors), connecting paper dolls with the name of a young woman in your ward written on each doll, or ornaments shaped like girls with the Young Women Theme written on each girl.

** May help fulfill a Beehive 2 Good Works Value Experience, a Mia Maid 1 Good Works Value Experience, a Mia Maid 1 Integrity Value Experience, and a Mia Maid 2 Good Works Value Experience*

Clay Sculpting

Each person uses a block of good clay and is assigned to sculpt another's face. Each person should have someone sculpting her. When the activity is over, everyone gets to take home an original sculpture of herself.

**May help fulfill a Mia Maid 1 Knowledge Value Experience and a Mia Maid 2 Knowledge Value Experience*

Donate Blood

Prior to this activity, arrange with your local hospital or blood bank to donate blood. After checking with the girls' parents and getting the necessary approval, take your class to the blood bank and donate blood.

** May help fulfill a Beehive 2 Good Works Value Experience, a Mia Maid 1 Good Works Value Experience, and a Mia Maid 2 Good Works Value Experience*

Family Traditions

For this activity, have each of the girls come prepared to tell about at least three of her family traditions. Let the young women share ideas of fun family traditions that the other girls might be able to start in their own families. Discuss the benefits of having family traditions. Be sensitive to any girls that might not have family traditions to share.

** Helps fulfill a Mia Maid 2 Individual Worth Value Experience*

Fingerprinting Service Project

For the first part of this activity, have a police officer or other professional teach your group how to properly take a fingerprint of someone. For the second part of this activity, perform a service project for members of your ward. Invite the Primary children of your ward to come to mutual with their parents so that you can fingerprint the children for identification purposes. Give the fingerprints to the children's parents to file for safekeeping.

** May help fulfill a Beehive 1 Good Works Value Experience, a Beehive 2 Good Works Value Experience, a Mia Maid 1 Good Works Value Experience, and a Mia Maid 2 Good Works Value Experience*

Fitness Center

Take your young women to a fitness center/exercise gym and work out together. Have a weight lifting instructor teach your group what machines work which muscles and how to properly use the equipment. Discuss the benefits of regular exercise. Also, discuss various techniques the girls can use to tone their muscles properly.

Handicap Awareness

Before holding this activity, make sure your girls understand the importance of respecting handicapped people. Set up the cultural hall of your ward meetinghouse like an obstacle course or a carnival in which your girls will participate. Then, give each girl a "handicap" by blindfolding her, giving her earplugs to wear, tying one of her arms and hands to her chest so they cannot be moved, providing her with crutches or a wheelchair which she must use, or taping her mouth shut. Then, instruct the girls to complete the obstacle course or carnival activities as best as she can with the handicap she has been given. After the girls have completed this part of the activity, remove the handicaps and discuss the benefits and the trials of handicaps and how important it is to be kind, sensitive, and helpful to those who deal with handicaps in their everyday lives. If possible, you should encourage someone with a disability to come and speak to the girls at this activity.

Handicap Helpers

Serve the parents of a handicapped child in your ward by teaching, feeding, or reading to the child. Another option would be to go to a state hospital and serve the handicapped people that live there. Help feed them, make crafts with them, or provide special physical stimulation and motivation to help them learn to walk or practice muscle coordination. If possible, do this more than once and keep a written or photographic history of what was done and how lives were affected by the activity.

** May help fulfill a Beehive 2 Divine Nature Value Experience, a Beehive 1 Good Works Value Experience, a Beehive 2 Good Works Value Experience, a Mia Maid 1 Good Works Value Experience, and a Mia Maid 2 Good Works Value Experience*

Variation: In order to make this a long-term project, make a schedule with your class. Between girls, take turns visiting the handicapped people on a regular basis. During the school year and even during the summer, you could take turns spending an hour each day providing this service. On a long-term program such as this one, you can really make a difference.

** May help fulfill a Beehive 2 Divine Nature Value Experience, a Beehive 1 Good Works Value Experience, a Beehive 2 Good Works Value Experience, a Mia Maid 1 Good Works Value Experience, and a Mia Maid 2 Good Works Value Experience*

Heritage Night

Assign each class member to research her ancestry to determine which country her ancestors came from. She is to prepare and bring a food item native to that country, as well as bring an heirloom from one of her ancestors to show to the class, if possible. For mutual, eat the international foods and take turns showing and telling about the heirlooms.

** Helps fulfill a Beehive 1 Individual Worth Value Experience and a Mia Maid 2 Individual Worth Value Experience*

Variation: Rather than researching a country, ask each girl to learn about a specific ancestor instead. Prior to this activity, have the girls each select one of her ancestors and learn as much as she can about that person. For mutual, let the girls share information about their ancestors' lives. Encourage them to bring photographs of their ancestors to display.

** Helps fulfill a Mia Maid 2 Individual Worth Value Experience*

Hobo Hangout

Come to this activity dressed like hobos and participate in "hobo" activities throughout the evening. Prior to this activity, you might even pass out invitations written on brown paper and each tucked into a small square of fabric tied to the end of a twig. Give the girls instructions to wear their oldest and baggiest clothing. Remind the girls that hobos were often adventurous people who wanted to travel, and were not necessarily homeless. Some activities you could participate in at this activity might be unscrambling words that relate to hobos (i.e. atrin = train, pemaficr = campfire, nadnanba = bandanna, tiurag = guitar), eating hobo dinners, going on a scavenger hunt for items necessary in the life of a hobo, telling stories around a campfire, and singing favorite songs with guitar accompaniment. Discuss how Heavenly Father loves all of His children individually, regardless of appearance, career, or lifestyle.

Hunter Safety

Sign the young women up to take a Hunter Safety class and certify in hunter safety. You will probably need to spend several consecutive mutual activities completing this activity. In order to set up this activity in advance, you will need to call your local Fish And Game office for the Hunter Safety class schedule for your area. Before scheduling this activity, be sure to obtain parental approval, since this activity involves the handling and shooting of guns.

I Have A Question

The *New Era* magazine contains a monthly section entitled, "I Have A Question," in which a question of the month is presented for readers to ponder and answer. Combine your thoughts and ideas as a Young Women class and put into words a response to the current month's question published in the magazine. Submit your answer to the *New Era* for possible publication. Additionally, send in any questions your girls may wish to have answered in future issues of the magazine.

Letters To Teachers

Let each girl in your group select at least two teachers who have been influential in her life and write letters to them. Have each girl express her thanks to these teachers and write several specific things she appreciates about what each teacher taught her. Design fancy stationery on which to write the letters, and enclose the letters in fancy envelopes that you have also designed. Then mail the letters.

** Helps fulfill a Beehive 2 Knowledge Value Experience and a Mia Maid 1 Individual Worth Value Experience*

Variation: Have each young woman write at least two letters to teenagers in your ward or stake who they admire as good examples of righteous living. Have them list specific qualities in the teenagers that they admire, and qualities in the teenagers that they wish to develop in themselves.

** Helps fulfill a Mia Maid 2 Individual Worth Value Experience*

Variation: Write letters to people who will soon be moving out of your ward. Mention how much you have enjoyed having them in your ward, the reasons you admire and will miss them, and your appreciation for their service in your behalf.

Life Stories

Split into groups of 2-3 girls per group, and visit some elderly people in the ward who would like some help recording their life histories. Each group takes a tape recorder, paper, pencils, and a list of good questions to get the stories rolling. Record the life histories for the first mutual activity and for a follow-up activity, type the histories and present them to their authors.

** May help fulfill a Beehive 1 Good Works Value Experience, a Beehive 2 Good Works Value Experience, a Mia Maid 1 Good Works Value Experience, a Mia Maid 2 Individual Worth Value Experience, and a Mia Maid 2 Good Works Value Experience*

Lifesaver Awards

This activity focuses on recognizing the good in others. Buy several packages of "Lifesavers" candies. Let the girls write one note to accompany each package of "Lifesavers," thanking different people for their examples or for kind acts of service that they have performed for others. In the notes, ask each of them to anonymously give a "Lifesaver Award" to someone else they admire. After you have made all of the awards, anonymously deliver the Lifesaver Awards.

Literacy Night

Read and record Church books or Church magazine articles onto cassette tapes. Donate them to members of your ward who cannot read for themselves because of illiteracy or physical impairment so they can listen to them, or give the tapes to your ward library to be filed and borrowed by interested ward members.

** May help fulfill a Beehive 1 Good Works Value Experience, a Beehive 2 Good Works Value Experience, a Mia Maid 1 Good Works Value Experience, and a Mia Maid 2 Good Works Value Experience*

Variation: Invite small children to your mutual activity and spend the evening reading good children's books to them. Another option would be to assign each girl in your class to read a good book and come prepared to report on it to the rest of the young women at a class book review.

Variation: Write simple children's stories and illustrate them by drawing appropriate pictures or by cutting appropriate pictures out of magazines and gluing them onto the pages of your books. Donate them to children or to your ward nursery closet.

** May help fulfill a Mia Maid 2 Good Works Value Experience*

Love Bucket

Start a "Love Bucket" in your ward. Obtain and decorate a bucket (a plastic ice cream bucket, a tin pail, or other bucket with handle). Fill the Love Bucket with fun items such as homemade goodies, uplifting stories, a copy of a Church magazine, stickers, a *Book of Mormon,* or a Church game. Include instructions to go along with the Love Bucket: the bucket must be delivered to a family in your ward during the first week of the month. That family gets to keep all of the ingredients in the bucket, and must replenish it with ingredients of the family's choice before secretly passing the bucket on to another ward family by the first week of the next month. As a class, select a family to deliver the Love Bucket to, and secretly deliver it as part of your activity.

Makeup Madness

All class members bring their makeup to this activity. Write each girl's name on a slip of paper and put all the slips of paper into a hat. Let each girl draw out a slip of paper and make sure she doesn't get her own name. The name she draws is the girl that gets to do her makeup for her that night. Let the girls do each other's makeup for the evening. Do each other's hair too, if time permits.

"My Turn On Earth"

Using the song "My Turn On Earth" by Carol Lynn Pearson and Lex De Azevedo as your theme, present an activity which centers on the youth of today and their important mission on earth in the latter days. Talks could focus on the plan of salvation, choosing the right, and the importance of making and keeping covenants, for example. Decorations could include clouds, angels, pictures of girls, temples, and even merry go rounds, if you decorate in keeping with the words of the theme song.

Parent Childhoods

Invite several parents of your young women to come and speak to your class about what life was like for them when they were children. Ask them to discuss their schools, their friends, their family traditions, and their chores, for example. Find out how technology has changed things during their lifetime. Encourage the young women to ask questions of the parents as well.

** Helps fulfill a Beehive 2 Individual Worth Value Experience*

Parent Spotlights

Ask one or both parents of each young woman to come to this activity prepared to present spotlights about their daughters. Invite them to bring any photographs, scrapbooks, or other items about their daughters that they wish to share. During the evening, let the parents take turns telling about their daughters. Have each set of parents share information about their daughter's special qualities, talents, interests, and personality. Give them a time limit if necessary.

** Helps fulfill a Beehive 2 Individual Worth Value Experience*

Patriarchal Blessings

Host a fireside in which the stake patriarch attends and gives a presentation on patriarchal blessings and then afterward answers questions from the youth. Ask him to talk about what patriarchal blessings are, why and when they are given, and what kinds of things young women can do to prepare to receive their blessings.

** Helps fulfill a Mia Maid 2 Individual Worth Value Experience and may help fulfill a Mia Maid 2 Knowledge Value Experience*

Pedigree Charts

Ask your ward family history consultant to address your class on the topic of genealogy. Have him explain what a pedigree chart is and what it is used for. Pass out pedigree charts to all class members and, with the help of the family history consultant, have each girl fill out her pedigree chart with as much information as possible. Request that the girls take their pedigree charts home and finish them with their parents.

** Helps fulfill a Beehive 1 Individual Worth Value Experience*

Variation: Fill out family group records instead of pedigree charts. Ask the ward family history consultant to give three family group records to each girl and to help them fill these records out as completely as they can. Each young woman should fill out one record with herself as a child, one with her father as a child, and one with her mother as a child.

** Helps fulfill a Beehive 2 Individual Worth Value Experience*

Personal Collages

Request each young woman to bring several old magazines that can be cut up and used in a collage. Provide a piece of posterboard for each young woman. Let the girls search through the magazines for pictures, words, and phrases that describe themselves such as their talents, hobbies, characteristics, personalities, and dreams. They should cut out the magazine clippings, arrange them on their pieces of posterboard, and then glue them on to make personal collages. When everyone is finished, take turns showing and explaining your collages to each other.

** Helps fulfill a Beehive 1 Individual Worth Value Experience*

Progressive Story Writing

Give each girl a blank piece of paper and a pencil. Have all the girls sit in a large circle, facing inward, and begin writing a story on their paper. After three minutes, all girls pass their stories one person to the left and continue writing the next part of the stories they just received. Continue in this fashion until every girl has written a section of every story. Then, read the stories aloud to each other.

Road Show

As a class, participate in a ward or stake road show together. Each girl should have a responsibility, either to act, direct, run the lighting, apply stage makeup, oversee the props, build scenery, design costumes, or operate the curtain.

** May help fulfill a Mia Maid 1 Individual Worth Value Experience*

Scrapbooks

Make scrapbooks together and let the girls fill them with various photographs, letters, and other memorabilia they have saved over the years. Remind the girls that scrapbooks should remind them of their past accomplishments, travels, friends, family, and life experiences. Encourage the girls to make scrapbooks that they and even their own children will enjoy looking at and learning from in future years.

** Helps fulfill a Mia Maid 1 Individual Worth Value Experience*

Searching For The Lost Piece of Silver

The emphasis for this activity is reactivation of the less active young women in your class. Focus on the importance of every young woman, including the girls who are less active in the Church. Stress that our Heavenly Father loves each of the young women in your class equally, and remind the girls that their responsibility is to search out every girl and make each one feel loved and accepted. Use the parable of the lost piece of silver found in Luke 15:8-9 as the theme for this activity.

** Helps fulfill a Beehive 1 Faith Value Experience*

X **Secret Granddaughters**

Have each young woman select an elderly man or woman in your ward for whom she will become a "secret granddaughter." During the year at various mutual activities, perform secret services for the "grandparents" such as delivering cupcakes, homemade rolls, and books to read, in addition to birthday cards on their birthdays. At the end of a year, host a party and invite the "grandparents" to attend. Let them know who their "secret granddaughters" are. At the party, the "grandparents" share their life histories with you.

X **Self Defense**

Ask a professional to come and speak to your girls about self defense and other personal safety issues for women. Teach the girls specific techniques for protecting themselves in dangerous circumstances. Discuss how to recognize and avoid potentially dangerous situations.

Service Coupons

Make coupons listing possible services that individual girls could offer to their families or other families in the ward. Some services you might offer: spring cleaning, cooking, painting, moving furniture, cleaning yards, planting, gardening, watering plants, mowing lawns, trimming shrubs, shoveling snow, weeding, babysitting, washing windows, scrubbing floors, wrapping gifts, or running errands. Pass the coupons out to family members or have a drawing at a ward function where families can draw service coupons to redeem in the future.

** May help fulfill a Beehive 1 Good Works Value Experience, a Beehive 2 Good Works Value Experience, and a Mia Maid 2 Good Works Value Experience*

X **Shopping For Shut-Ins**

Select one or two shut-in ward members who would appreciate your doing their weekly shopping for them. Have them prepare lists of needed items and give their money to your leader. For mutual, purchase the items and deliver them to the shut-in members.

** Helps fulfill a Mia Maid 1 Good Works Value Experience and may help fulfill a Beehive 1 Good Works Value Experience, a Beehive 2 Good Works Value Experience, a Mia Maid 1 Good Works Value Experience, and a Mia Maid 2 Good Works Value Experience*

Variation: Read to shut-ins instead. Contact the selected ward members prior to this activity and get ideas for what types of books they enjoy. Then for the activity, check out the desired books from your local library, go to their homes, and read to them.

** May help fulfill a Beehive 1 Good Works Value Experience, a Beehive 2 Good Works Value Experience, a Mia Maid 1 Good Works Value Experience, and a Mia Maid 2 Good Works Value Experience*

Sign Language

Have someone who knows American Sign Language come to your class and teach some sign language to you. You could learn some basic phrases, the words to a song or Church hymn, or the Young Women Theme in American Sign Language.

X **Spotlights**

Prior to this activity, put all the girls' names into a hat and have them each draw a name out of the hat, making sure no girl gets her own name. She is to read the name she drew and work with the mother of that girl to create a spotlight about the girl. She should focus on getting information about the girl's hobbies, interests, talents, and goals. For mutual, each girl gives the spotlight about the young woman she has chosen. If time permits, you could allow the other girls to ask the spotlighted girl questions after she is spotlighted. Have each young woman make and give her spotlighted girl a piece of the latter's favorite dessert.

> **Variation:** Get a piece of paper for each girl in your class and write one girl's name on the top of each paper. Provide a pencil or pen for every young woman. For mutual, pass the papers around the class and let everyone write one quality she admires most about the girl named at the top of the paper. When everyone has written one quality about each of the others, read the papers aloud.

> **Variation:** Everyone brings a baby picture of herself. Each person also brings information on another young woman who she is prepared to spotlight. Each person shares her spotlight without revealing the name of the girl being spotlighted, and the other girls write on a piece of paper who they think each one is. After all of the girls have presented their spotlights, reveal who's who.

Thank You Notes

Write thank you notes to individuals that you are grateful for and state in the notes why you appreciate them. Some people you might write notes to are your Congressman, your bishop, your mayor, or your parents.

** Helps fulfill a Mia Maid 1 Individual Worth Value Experience*

Variation: Write thank you notes to the management of a television or radio station in your area that sponsors quality programs or music for its viewers or listeners. In the letters, tell them how important you believe good media is to your community and how much you appreciate their willingness to provide it for their viewers.

** Helps fulfill a Mia Maid 2 Integrity Value Experience*

Ward Talent Book

As a class, compile a book of original talks, short stories, recipes, artwork, and poetry written by members of your ward. You might categorize the book by topic, by type of contribution, or by last name alphabetically. Make copies available to interested ward members.

Worth of A Soul

Each girl brings her *Book of Mormon* to mutual. Divide into groups and assign each group several chapters in 3 Nephi, specifically 3 Nephi 11 - 20. If you desire, you can also read *Doctrine and Covenants* 18:10 and John 13:34. Have the groups read their chapters together, searching for anything that indicates the worth of a soul. Hold a discussion about what you find.

** May help fulfill a Mia Maid 1 Individual Worth Value Experience*

chapter four

Knowledge

Airport Visit

Visit a large airport. Teach the young women how to check flight schedules, find terminals, check in, and obtain their baggage from the baggage claim. Ask an airport employee to explain how baggage checking and baggage claims work, to discuss airport security measures, and to give some travel tips, if possible.

Art Museum

Visit an art museum together as a class. Look at the different types of art and discuss biographies of some prominent artists.

Astronomy

Study astronomy together by checking out books from the library or asking someone familiar with this field to come and speak to the girls. If possible, set up a telescope and take turns looking at constellations and other heavenly bodies. If a telescope is unavailable, use binoculars. For a great Gospel discussion during this activity, read and discuss Abraham 3:1-14 together.

Auto Maintenance

Have an auto mechanic give a presentation to your class about basic auto care. Ask him to teach you how to change a flat tire, check the oil, change the oil, replace a fuse, and check the tire pressure, for example.

**May help fulfill a Mia Maid 1 Knowledge Value Experience and a Mia Maid 2 Knowledge Value Experience*

Boating

After making sure your young women are proficient swimmers and after getting permission from the girls' parents, go boating together. Learn the names and functions of the different parts of a boat and how to operate a boat properly. Show the girls how to properly prepare a boat before boating and how to properly clean and prepare a boat for storage. Teach the girls boat safety rules and the rescue procedures to use if someone were to fall overboard.

Cake Decorating

Ask a professional cake decorator to come and teach your Young Women class about the art of cake decorating. Have a few cakes available to decorate, and give each girl a turn decorating them. Deliver finished cakes to families in your area who are in need of special cheer.

**May help fulfill a Mia Maid 1 Knowledge Value Experience and a Mia Maid 2 Knowledge Value Experience*

Campfire Building

Go to an outdoor area that would be conducive to building campfires and practice building at least three different types of small, safe campfires. Discuss the importance of kindling, tinder, fire safety, and fire containment. Show how to collect, protect, and use wood on a rainy day. Illustrate the different methods of lighting a fire, such as using matches or flint and steel. If time permits, practice cooking over a campfire and adjusting campfire heat. Obtain a fire permit beforehand if necessary.

** May help fulfill a Mia Maid 1 Knowledge Value Experience and a Mia Maid 2 Knowledge Value Experience*

Christmas In July

Host a Christmas craft fair sometime in July. Display several cute Christmas crafts and teach the girls to make several of them. You will all feel less stressed when Christmas time approaches and you have several gifts and crafts already made!

** May help fulfill a Beehive 1 Knowledge Value Experience and a Beehive 2 Good Works Value Experience*

College Panel

Invite several trustworthy college students to come to this activity and sit on a college panel which allows your youth to ask them questions about college and which lets the college students give your girls advice for making the transition from high school to college life as smooth as possible. Questions might cover topics such as study habits, finances, social life, Institute, and living on your own. To locate some good college students to help you with this activity, consider asking the council members of your area's Institute program.

College Tour

Go on a tour of a college or university in your area to see what facilities can be taken advantage of by the girls right now, before they graduate from high school.

Look at places like the campus library, the bookstore, and the fine arts center. Help the girls become familiar with a college campus in order to help them make a smooth transition from high school to college. Discuss the many differences between high school and college life.

Creative Cookery

Divide your class into two or more groups. Give each group a sack or box filled with ingredients to make a meal. You can choose to include or leave out a recipe. Let the groups prepare the meal together from the ingredients found in their sacks or boxes.

** May help fulfill a Mia Maid 1 Knowledge Value Experience and a Mia Maid 2 Knowledge Value Experience*

Cultural Refinement

As a class, study ballet or opera together, and then attend a performance together. To make this idea work on a more limited budget, consider attending a matinee performance or even a dress rehearsal, which may be less expensive or even free.

** Helps fulfill a Beehive 1 Knowledge Value Experience and a Beehive 2 Knowledge Value Experience*

Dance Lessons

Teach the girls how to square dance or do the waltz, the polka, ballet, or line dancing. You might arrange to have a professional dancer come to your class and teach the girls. It might be appropriate to invite the young men to participate with you in this activity by becoming dance partners for the girls.

Engineering

Contact a local engineering office and ask an employee to give your class an on site tour of one of their current construction projects. As part of the tour, ask the engineer to show the blueprints or other drawings from which the project is being built.

**May help fulfill a Mia Maid 1 Knowledge Value Experience and a Mia Maid 2 Knowledge Value Experience*

Farm Visit

While visiting a farm may not be too exciting to a farmer's child, it is highly educational for "city girls" to see where many of the products come from that they eat and how they are produced. Arrange with the owner or manager of a farm or ranch to allow the young women to get some hands-on experience working on a farm and ask questions about what it takes to run the farm, including ways to market his products. The girls might be able to bottle-feed calves, milk cows or goats, slop pigs, learn to drive a tractor, or shear sheep, for starters.

**May help fulfill a Mia Maid 1 Knowledge Value Experience and a Mia Maid 2 Knowledge Value Experience*

Fire Station

Take your girls to your local fire station. Ask the fire chief to explain the different types of fires and the uses of the fire equipment and fire trucks located at the fire station. Discuss the fire prevention activities in your community and suggest ways the girls can be involved in fire prevention.

**May help fulfill a Mia Maid 1 Knowledge Value Experience and a Mia Maid 2 Knowledge Value Experience*

First Aid Instruction

Take the girls to the local red cross chapter for CPR (Cardiopulmonary Resuscitation) classes, and let them certify in CPR. Another option would be to ask a certified CPR instructor to come to your ward and teach the girls first aid techniques at your ward meetinghouse.

**May help fulfill a Mia Maid 1 Knowledge Value Experience and a Mia Maid 2 Knowledge Value Experience*

First Aid Kits

Invite a nurse or other medical professional to show the girls what types of things would go in a home first aid kit or a travel first aid kit. Display several types of kits and suggest ways that the girls can make simple first aid supplies at home to put in their own first aid kits. If time permits, let the girls make some supplies as part of the activity, such as large bandages or cravats made out of clean white sheets.

Global Church

Assign each young woman a country to research and provide appropriate research aids for the activity such as books, maps, Church magazines, and copies of the *Church News*. The girls should seek information on the history of the Church in the country she is assigned. After everyone is finished researching, each youth should briefly teach the others what she has learned. All of the young women could come to this activity dressed in clothing from a foreign country, if you desire.

Gospel On Computer

Meet at a ward member's home who has access to Church-related computer programs and is willing to demonstrate how to use them. The program disks may contain the scriptures, General Conference reports, or religious clip art, for example. Learn how these programs can help you study about Gospel topics, prepare sacrament meeting talks, study the scriptures, and increase your Gospel knowledge.

Grocery Store Visit

Pre-arrange with the manager of a local grocery store or supermarket to tour the facility for mutual. The young women should each bring a list of questions to ask the manager about the management of a grocery store. Questions could be about how things are priced, how often shipments are received, what factors are affected when certain store items go on sale, customer satisfaction policies, and division of labor among employees, for example. The tour might include going behind the scenes to the grocery store warehouse to view the freezers, refrigerators, receiving bays, and the manager's office, if permitted.

**May help fulfill a Mia Maid 1 Knowledge Value Experience and a Mia Maid 2 Knowledge Value Experience*

Higher Education

Bring a guest speaker to this mutual activity to address the value of higher education. The speaker should speak for about 20-25 minutes and for the rest of the evening answer such questions as how to apply for college, what prerequisites are needed for admission to different college programs, and the value of the Institute program of the Church. Discuss financial aid options such as academic scholarships, departmental scholarships, government grants, and school loans. Remember to talk about trade schools as well as colleges.

Historical Landmark

Visit a historical landmark in your area such as a famous battleground, a historical building, the home of a famous person, a pioneer trail, or a religious building. Teach your class about the events which took place at that location to make it a historical landmark, and talk about the impact this area has had on your local history.

Home Repairs

Learn basic home repairs including how to replace a faucet washer, check the circuit breaker box, repair a plug, unclog a sink or drain, or hang a picture. Also, learn how to shut off the electricity, water, and gas during an emergency.

**May help fulfill a Mia Maid 1 Knowledge Value Experience and a Mia Maid 2 Knowledge Value Experience*

Horse Care

For this activity, arrange with a horse owner to meet at his stable and allow him to teach your girls how to properly care for a horse. He should teach them how to groom, feed, saddle, clean, bridle, mount, and lead a horse, and could show them the difference between a trot, a canter, a gallop, and a run. If possible, let the girls take turns saddling and riding the horse as part of the activity.

**May help fulfill a Mia Maid 1 Knowledge Value Experience and a Mia Maid 2 Knowledge Value Experience*

Industrial Plant

Visit an industrial plant that either makes chemical products or uses chemical processes to make other products. Ask an employee of the plant to tell your girls why chemicals are used in that type of business and what types of careers are available to chemists, chemical engineers, and chemical technicians. Discuss the pollutants created by chemicals and ways that the company attempts to minimize the dangers of chemical pollutants.

**May help fulfill a Mia Maid 1 Knowledge Value Experience and a Mia Maid 2 Knowledge Value Experience*

International Dinner

Assign each girl in your class to bring a part of a meal featuring cuisine from another country. Dress up like natives of that country and have an international dinner together. If desired, you can assign certain class members to prepare oral reports about the country and present them to the class while you eat.

Jail Visit

Arrange to visit a jail or prison. Have each of the girls fingerprinted, and ask a prison employee to teach the girls basic fingerprinting skills and different types of fingerprint patterns. Discuss how the fingerprinting process helps the police find and catch criminals. Let a police officer pretend to "book" and "handcuff" the young women and give them a tour of the jail. Ask the officer to tell your group what it is like to be a police officer and what it is like to be in prison.

**May help fulfill a Mia Maid 1 Knowledge Value Experience and a Mia Maid 2 Knowledge Value Experience*

Jewelry Making

Make jewelry together. If possible, let a skilled class member teach this class. You could make braided necklaces, leather jewelry, beaded earrings, or wooden bracelets, for example.

** May help fulfill a Beehive 1 Knowledge Value Experience, a*

Beehive 2 Good Works Value Experience, a Mia Maid 1 Knowledge Value Experience, and a Mia Maid 2 Knowledge Value Experience

Machine Shop Visit

Arrange to visit a machine shop in your community. Ask a machinist to give your group a tour of the facility, explaining different machines and their uses. Discuss how technological advances have affected the machining industry. Discuss also the safety precautions taken in the shop, including protective clothing and protective eye wear.

**May help fulfill a Mia Maid 1 Knowledge Value Experience and a Mia Maid 2 Knowledge Value Experience*

Mortuary Visit

Visit a mortuary and let the mortician give you a tour of the facility. Have him teach your girls about his profession and how the deceased are properly cared for by those in this business.

**May help fulfill a Mia Maid 1 Knowledge Value Experience and a Mia Maid 2 Knowledge Value Experience*

Music Melodies

Spend the activity learning about music. Some ideas: learn how to conduct music, learn basics about playing a musical instrument, learn a Church song or hymn to perform in sacrament meeting, or learn how to read music. You might also let the girls play in a "homemade orchestra," where each girl must bring something from home that can be used as an instrument but is not really a musical instrument, such as shakers, spoons, nails in a can, a pan, or a pie tin. Play your instruments together in a "homemade orchestra" and possibly later in a ward talent show.

** May help fulfill a Beehive 1 Faith Value Experience, a Mia Maid 1 Individual Worth Value Experience, a Mia Maid 1 Knowledge Value Experience, and a Mia Maid 2 Knowledge Value Experience*

New Era Bowl

Each girl brings at least one *New Era* magazine, or get several *New Era* magazines from the ward library. Give one magazine to each girl and take 20-30 minutes to let the girls search through their magazines to come up with several trivia questions for which the answers are found in the *New Era*. Let the girls write these questions and answers on a piece of paper or on several index cards. After the 20-30 minutes have expired, play *New Era* Bowl, a game where each girl takes turns reading one of her questions to the group to see who can answer it. Play as individuals or as teams.

** Helps fulfill a Beehive 1 Knowledge Value Experience and may help fulfill a Mia Maid 2 Choice And Accountability Value Experience*

Variation: Play *Church News* Bowl following the same rules as for *New Era* Bowl, but use recent issues of the *Church News* instead of the *New Era* to find trivia questions. This is a good way to learn about current events in the Church.

Orienteering

This activity helps the girls prepare for Girl's Camp. Require each girl to bring a compass. Learn how to read compasses together. Go outside and record the direction of the sun at sunset, and learn how to find your way when you are lost by using a compass as a navigational tool.

Variation: Set up an orienteering treasure hunt for your girls with five markers that they have to find. Prepare a master map, mark the descriptive clues, make sure each girl has a compass, and let them use their compasses to find the markers and the treasure you have placed at the end of the hunt.

Photography

Ask each girl to bring her camera and film to this activity. Go to a location where a variety of nice photographs could be taken such as a lakeside, a mountain, a bird refuge, or a park. Talk about what makes a good photograph and then let the girls practice by taking pictures of the surrounding area. You might want to invite a professional photographer to come to this activity with your girls and talk about what makes a good picture. He could discuss lighting, film speed, shutter speed, and angles, for example.

** Helps fulfill a Beehive 1 Knowledge Value Experience, a Mia Maid 1 Knowledge Value Experience, and a Mia Maid 2 Knowledge Value Experience*

Pioneer Cooking

Dress up like pioneer women and cook a full pioneer meal outdoors over a campfire. Teach your girls techniques the pioneers used for cooking their meals on the trail. Discuss the types of food they cooked and the types of fuel they used when wood was hard to find.

** May help fulfill a Mia Maid 1 Knowledge Value Experience and a Mia Maid 2 Knowledge Value Experience*

Plant Care

Ask a botanist or other expert on plants to come and speak to your group about how to properly care for indoor and outdoor plants. Learn what plants grow well in your area, how to properly grow a garden, how to maintain a garden throughout the seasons, how to start plants by seeds, roots, cuttings, and tubers, and how to control pests.

**May help fulfill a Mia Maid 1 Knowledge Value Experience and a Mia Maid 2 Knowledge Value Experience*

Poetry Writing

Teach the girls to write poetry, and then let them experiment by writing several poems of their own. Make sure you teach a variety of poetry forms and remember that poems don't always have to rhyme. Some examples of poetry types you could teach are limericks, haiku, and free verse.

**May help fulfill a Mia Maid 1 Knowledge Value Experience and a Mia Maid 1 Good Works Value Experience*

Postal Service

Visit your local post office or mail handling annex. Tour the facility, noting the different jobs and machines used to process mail quickly and efficiently. See how employees handle mail, track package destinations, and use security measures to detect dangerous packages such as mail bombs. Ask the manager of the facility to describe the various careers available in the postal service.

**May help fulfill a Mia Maid 1 Knowledge Value Experience and a Mia Maid 2 Knowledge Value Experience*

Printing Establishment

Visit a printing establishment in your area. Let the printer show you how paper is used in the printing business. Ask him to demonstrate the process of printing a book or newspaper and teach your group the history of papermaking and bookbinding. Talk to him about careers in the fields of printing and graphic arts.

**May help fulfill a Mia Maid 1 Knowledge Value Experience and a Mia Maid 2 Knowledge Value Experience*

Variation: Visit a book publishing company. Find out what steps a book must go through in order to become published and if possible, view books in each phase of the publication process. Learn what is involved in writing and editing an original manuscript, designing a book layout and cover, and in printing, distributing, and marketing the books. Ask a publisher how he recognizes a good manuscript and what factors he uses in determining whether to accept or reject a manuscript for publication.

**May help fulfill a Mia Maid 1 Knowledge Value Experience and a Mia Maid 2 Knowledge Value Experience*

Progressive Dinner And Etiquette Night

Assign each class to prepare one course of a three course meal (example: Beehives = appetizer, Mia Maids = main course, Laurels = dessert). Set up each course in a different room of the Church meetinghouse and have a progressive dinner together. Lead your entire group of girls to the first room where appetizers are served. While the girls are eating their appetizers, teach them proper etiquette for eating the particular foods you have served. When the girls have finished their appetizers, move to the next room for the main course. While they eat the main course, speak to the girls again about the importance of proper etiquette and give them specific suggestions for eating their meal appropriately. Finally, take them to the last room for dessert, and teach proper manners for that course as well. When you are finished with this activity, the girls will not only have full stomachs, but they will also have better manners. Some food ideas that tend to be difficult to eat politely which you may want to serve at this activity are spaghetti, shrimp, and artichokes.

Radiology

Visit a radiologist's laboratory. Learn the variety of ways that X-rays are used in today's world. Discuss safety codes, special equipment and dress, and possible dangers of X-ray radiation. Ask the radiologist about educational requirements and career opportunities in the field of radiology and about the future of radiology.

**May help fulfill a Mia Maid 1 Knowledge Value Experience and a Mia Maid 2 Knowledge Value Experience*

Restaurant Visit

Arrange a visit to a restaurant. Tour the kitchen area and see how different menu items are prepared. Meet with the owner or manager and allow the young women to ask questions about the business of running a restaurant. Each young woman should have a list of questions she plans to ask the restaurant owner, which could be about federal regulations and inspections, quality control, getting the food to the restaurant, cooking methods, and properly washing the dishes and other restaurant equipment. After talking with the manager, order dessert or a meal at the restaurant, depending on what your finances and time restrictions allow.

**May help fulfill a Mia Maid 1 Knowledge Value Experience and a Mia Maid 2 Knowledge Value Experience*

Scripture Bee

Have a spelling bee using names of people, places, and

things in the scriptures. To add variety, you may allow the girls to spin a dial or roll a die to determine which category the word will come from, such as *Old Testament, New Testament, Book of Mormon, Doctrine and Covenants,* or *Pearl of Great Price.*

Search And Rescue Instruction

With the help of a professional Search And Rescue worker, instruct the girls in emergency rescue procedures. If it would be feasible and safe, this activity could be done on site, for example in a mountain or near a river. Stress the importance of exercising safety and caution in all situations.

> **Variation:** Learn safety rules for specific emergency situations you may encounter in your area, such as floods, earthquakes, tornadoes, hurricanes, mud slides, or drought. Another idea would be to talk about specific safety rules for women and children, what to do if a child is missing, how to protect yourself and the children in your care when you babysit, or accident prevention.

Swimming

After making sure your girls are proficient swimmers, go swimming together as a group. You could go to a public or private swimming pool or, after verifying the safety of the location and after getting any necessary permission, go to a pond, lake, river, or ocean. While there, practice several types of swimming strokes, dives, life saving techniques, and water rescue techniques. If time permits, you could play water basketball or water polo together.

✓Teen Cuisine

Spend an activity learning how to cook and prepare at least five nutritious meals that can be easily prepared by a teenager. Focus on easy breakfasts, lunches, after school snacks, dinners, and desserts, and make sure the girls write down the recipes for future use.

**May help fulfill a Beehive 2 Knowledge Value Experience, a Mia Maid 1 Knowledge Value Experience, and a Mia Maid 2 Knowledge Value Experience*

Telephone Etiquette

Teach your class proper telephone etiquette. Discuss the proper way to answer a telephone at home and on the job. Practice answering phones properly and handling difficult telephone encounters politely and appropriately.

Television Station Visit

With permission, visit a local television station. Take a tour of the different departments and ask the manager to explain how the staff works together to produce quality television programming. If possible, watch the recording of a local news broadcast.

**May help fulfill a Mia Maid 1 Knowledge Value Experience and a Mia Maid 2 Knowledge Value Experience*

Variation: With permission, visit a local radio station instead and quietly watch the production of a live radio station broadcast. If possible, tour the facility.

**May help fulfill a Mia Maid 1 Knowledge Value Experience and a Mia Maid 2 Knowledge Value Experience*

Textile Plant

Visit a textile plant. Tour the facility and learn about the various types of fiber and how they are harvested or produced. Learn also the steps for making fiber into cloth. Compare several different types of fabric, such as waterproof tent material, breathable material for sportswear, and T-shirt material. Ask how textile products are marketed and what factors affect the pricing of these products. Discuss the different types of jobs available in the textile industry.

**May help fulfill a Mia Maid 1 Knowledge Value Experience and a Mia Maid 2 Knowledge Value Experience*

Treasure of Knowledge

Make sure the young women bring their scriptures to this activity. Before the activity begins, prepare a treasure hunt for the girls. Write clues in the form of scriptural references, each containing the book of scripture, the chapter, and the verse where the answer to the clue can be found. At the activity, give the girls the first clue. They must look up the required scripture to find the answer. The answer is the location where the second clue is hidden. (Example: *Doctrine And Covenants* 88:118, "Seek ye out of the best books," could lead the girls to the ward library, 2 Nephi 9:51, "And feast upon that which perisheth not," could lead them to the kitchen, and Moroni 7:11, "A bitter fountain cannot bring forth good water," could lead them to the drinking fountain. The girls must follow the clues through the church building to a treasure which you have hidden at the end of the hunt.

Veterinarian Visit

Set up a visit with a veterinarian. Ask him to show you procedures which he uses on animals and explain basic care for different types of animals. If possible, tour his office and view the equipment, holding pens, and various rooms. Discuss educational requirements and job opportunities for veterinarians.

**May help fulfill a Mia Maid 1 Knowledge Value Experience and a Mia Maid 2 Knowledge Value Experience*

Waste Treatment Plant

Visit a waste treatment plant in your area. Tour the facility, noting how waste is disposed of properly and what measures are taken to treat, dispose of, and recycle waste products. Discuss the importance of keeping the earth free from excessive waste and give tips for conserving resources and recycling products.

**May help fulfill a Mia Maid 1 Knowledge Value Experience and a Mia Maid 2 Knowledge Value Experience*

Waterskiing

During the long, sunlit days of summer, take the young women to a lake and arrange with a ward member who has a boat and waterskiing equipment to teach the young women how to waterski. Before skiing, instruct the girls in boat safety and water safety. Discuss waterskiing equipment and techniques and then give the girls a chance to try waterskiing.

Weaving

Learn to weave together. You could weave baskets, doormats, or place mats. To personalize your work, you might try weaving your family name into the doormat or set of place mats with a different color to make it stand out.

Weed Salad

Using the *Boy Scout Handbook* or other reliable source,

find out what local weeds are edible in your area. Stroll through the countryside collecting edible weeds together. A cooler with ice and/or water will help keep the weeds fresh through the stroll. After your walk, return to the church and prepare a large weed salad to share.

Woodworking

This activity works best if it takes place at a wood shop. Under the guidance of a carpenter, discuss different types of wood and wood tools. Let each of the girls in your class design and make something useful out of wood.

** Helps fulfill a Beehive 1 Knowledge Value Experience and may help fulfill a Beehive 2 Good Works Value Experience, a Mia Maid 1 Knowledge Value Experience, and a Mia Maid 2 Knowledge Value Experience*

chapter five

Choice & Accountability

Abuse Awareness And Prevention

Ask a speaker to come and speak to the girls about the dangers of abuse (physical, emotional, and sexual) and how to avoid relationships and situations where they might be abused. List the personality traits which are warning signs of a potential abuser and suggest ways the girls can protect themselves from getting into dangerous relationships. Give tips on how to get out of abusive relationships.

**May help fulfill a Mia Maid 2 Choice And Accountability Value Experience*

Bible Dictionary Game

Provide pencils and paper for the young women and request that they bring their Bibles to this activity. To begin playing this game, one of the young women searches through her Bible Dictionary for a word for which no one in your group knows the definition. She announces the word to the group, spelling it if necessary, and all players write the word on their paper. While she writes the correct definition for the word, the other players must invent their own definitions, making them sound as believable as possible. When everyone has finished writing their definitions, she collects the papers and reads the definitions aloud. All players but the young woman reading the definitions vote individually for whichever definition they think is correct. She then announces the correct definition and scores the round. If a player guessed the right definition, she scores one point. If player #1 chooses player #2's made up definition, player #2 gets a point for fooling her. After everyone gets the proper amount of points, another girl chooses a dictionary word and play resumes as before.

Biographies

For this activity, bring books and magazines that the girls in your class could use to learn about the life of a prominent person in Church history, or check appropriate books and magazines out from your ward library. Include the scriptures, *Ensign* magazines, and a variety of Church books in your selection. Let each girl select a person to learn about and spend the first part of the activity researching about the selected individuals, focusing on the choices the person made and the impact those choices had upon society. Then, take turns presenting what you have learned to each other. Discuss that person's contributions to society and the impact the person has had on society throughout history.

** Helps fulfill a Beehive 1 Knowledge Value Experience*

Budget Cooking

Give each young woman $1.00 from the Young Women's budget and take the girls to the local grocery store. Instruct the girls to purchase enough ingredients with their dollars to each make a simple dessert. Then, go back to the church and in the ward kitchen, let the girls prepare their desserts and share them with the rest of the class.

**May help fulfill a Mia Maid 1 Knowledge Value Experience and a Mia Maid 2 Knowledge Value Experience*

X **Candy Bar Exchange**

Provide an assortment of candy bars for this activity. Give one to each girl to begin. The goal for this activity is for each person to end up with the kind of candy bar she wants. Have all participants sit around a table and show each other their candy bars, and then hide their candy bars on their laps. Choose a person to begin the game and select a "lucky number" to be rolled with two dice. The starting person rolls the dice, hoping to get the lucky number. If she doesn't, the dice are passed one person to the left and that person rolls them. If she does get the lucky number, she states the name of a candy bar and who she believes has that kind of candy bar. If she is correct, she gets to switch candy bars with that person, and the dice are passed one person to the left. Continue doing this for a certain time period or until everyone has the kind of candy bar she wanted.

Career Choices

Ask your ward or stake employment specialist or professionals from certain careers to come and speak to your class. Ask them to discuss what they do at their jobs, what they enjoy about their work, and what their occupations contribute to society. Some career choices to consider: woodworking, auto mechanics, firefighting, taxidermy, sales, law, child development, engineering, homemaking, photography, geology, pottery making, jewelry making, medicine, computer science, and teaching.

**Helps fulfill a Mia Maid 1 Knowledge Value Experience and a Mia Maid 2 Knowledge Value Experience*

Carnival of Life

Set up the cultural hall of your ward meetinghouse to resemble a carnival. Give the girls each a small bag and some tickets. The girls can use their tickets to play any of the games which you have set up at the carnival. Some of the games are worldly (basketball toss) and some are spiritual (name that Apostle). The worldly games give pennies to the winners, and the spiritual games give tokens to the winners. Send an adult leader around the room to silently escort the girls out of the carnival one at a time. She escorts the girls to another room of the ward meetinghouse where the bishop or bishopric member (dressed in white) waits to judge her. He counts her tokens and based on the amount earned, sentences her to one of the three kingdoms: Celestial, Terrestrial, or Telestial. Once all of the girls have been sentenced and taken to the proper kingdom, give a short fireside on the importance of proper choices in this "carnival of life."

City Council Meeting

Attend a local city council meeting to see how your local government works and what issues they present, debate, and vote upon. Take notes, develop opinions about the issues facing your community, and after the meeting is over, talk about what you have learned. Discuss the value of having a city council, the importance of public opinion, and the organization of the council. As a class or individually, write letters to the chairman of your city council expressing your opinions.

** May help fulfill a Beehive 1 Knowledge Value Experience and a Beehive 2 Knowledge Value Experience*

Collecting

Ask several ward members to display and tell about their collections. With a little investigation, you will probably find a large number of collectors in your own ward with interesting collections of many kinds. Give suggestions to the girls for starting their own collections. Some common collectible items are: coins, stamps, spoons, dolls, comic books, rocks, and baseball cards. Let the girls ask questions of the collectors.

Creative Pizzas

Have a creative pizza party. Provide the dough and let each girl roll out her own crust. Make several topping choices available, and let the girls design their own pizzas. See who can come up with the most unusual or attractive pizzas. Cook them and eat together.

**May help fulfill a Mia Maid 1 Knowledge Value Experience and a Mia Maid 2 Knowledge Value Experience*

Employment Office

Visit an employment office. Talk about the concerns of working people such as job security, job safety, job satisfaction, seniority, wages, benefits, and working conditions. Help the young women understand that each job has pros and cons, and give suggestions to help the young women select jobs that fit their individual needs, talents, and desires.

Exercise

Do aerobics or another work out routine together. Ask a qualified instructor to come and teach the routine to your girls, or use a good exercise video as your guide.

**May help fulfill a Beehive 1 Knowledge Value Experience and a Beehive 2 Knowledge Value Experience*

Extemporaneous Speaking

This activity helps the young women develop their abilities to speak in front of a crowd. Bring several current national news magazines and select article topics that could serve as subjects for short speeches. Allow each young woman to choose a topic and prepare a 5-8 minute speech about it using the magazines provided. If you desire, you can provide index cards for taking notes. After the girls have finished preparing, let them give their speeches to one another.

**May help fulfill a Mia Maid 1 Individual Worth Value Experience and a Mia Maid 2 Knowledge Value Experience*

Variation: Outline the qualities that make a good sacrament meeting talk. Prepare and practice giving 5-8 minute talks on various Gospel subjects to each other.

**Helps fulfill a Beehive 2 Knowledge Value Experience and may help fulfill a Mia Maid 1 Individual Worth Value Experience and a Mia Maid 2 Knowledge Value Experience*

Fire!

Begin this activity with the young women in the cultural hall of your ward building. Stage a pretend "fire" and tell the girls that the building has burned down and you all have died. Escort the girls to another room in the building (possibly the Relief Society room) where the three members of the bishopric sit, wearing all white clothing. Sit down and listen to the bishopric as they give a fireside about life, death, and judgment. Ask them to talk about the different requirements for attaining the three kingdoms of heaven and why it is important to make good choices now, before this life and its opportunities are over.

Possible refreshments following this activity might be devil's food cake and angel food cake.

> **Variation:** Set up the cultural hall like the interior of an airplane. The Young Women leaders should dress up like flight attendants. Let the girls come in, sit down, put on their seatbelts, and prepare for takeoff. Simulate an airplane crash and then after announcing that everyone has died, escort the girls to another room in the building (possibly the Relief Society room) where the three members of the bishopric sit, wearing all white clothing. Sit down and listen to the bishopric as they give a fireside about life, death, and judgment.

Gospel Feud

Let the young women think of several Gospel questions and then call ward members on the telephone to ask them to answer the questions. Count the answers given and determine the five answers which were most frequently given for each question. Then, play Gospel Feud together (possibly with the young men their age). Divide the youth into two equal teams and sit them on either side of a room with a leader at a small table in the middle of the room. Another leader writes the top five answers for the first question on the chalkboard and covers them with five large strips of posterboard. The first player on each team comes to the center table and faces the other, and the leader asks the first question. Example: "Out of ___ people surveyed, the top five answers are on the chalkboard. Here's the question. Name an animal mentioned in the *Book of Mormon*." The first player to hit the table gets to answer the question. If she answers correctly, she scores a point, her answer is revealed on the chalkboard, and her team members take turns guessing the rest of the answers. If she answers incorrectly, the other player at the table guesses. If he answers correctly, he gets a point, his answer is revealed on the chalkboard, and his team members take turns guessing the rest of the answers. When a team member guesses a correct answer, she scores a point for her team. If she does not answer correctly, she gets a strike. If the team gets three strikes, play passes to the other team who tries to name the answers. After all five answers have been revealed, erase them and play again using the second question surveyed.

Healthy Budget

This activity will require two mutual nights to complete. For the first mutual night, take the girls to a local grocery store and give each girl paper, a pencil, and a pretend $20.00 budget. Instruct them each to make a three day menu which would feed two people three meals a day while staying within their budget. They should give you their lists at the end of the first activity. For the next week, ask a nurse or health practitioner to visit your class and give a short presentation on the importance of health and nutrition. Ask her to check the girls' menus for health content and talk to the girls about eating healthy on a limited budget.

**May help fulfill a Beehive 2 Knowledge Value Experience, a Mia Maid 1 Knowledge Value Experience, and a Mia Maid 2 Knowledge Value Experience*

Home Decorating

Learn about home decorating including the use of color, balance, harmony, and proportion. Provide several different objects which could be used in decorating, such as plants, pictures, mirrors, and collectibles. Let the young women practice arranging and decorating with them.

**May help fulfill a Mia Maid 1 Knowledge Value Experience and a Mia Maid 2 Knowledge Value Experience*

Variation: Learn how to wallpaper a room. Ask a professional to show your class how to hang wallpaper properly. Show the different types of wallpapering tools and talk about the various qualities of wallpaper and wallpaper borders for sale.

**May help fulfill a Mia Maid 1 Knowledge Value Experience and a Mia Maid 2 Knowledge Value Experience*

Library Visit

As a class, visit your county library. Ask a librarian to give your group a tour of the facility, explaining the various resources available at the library. Use the computer and the card catalog to find the location of a specific book, and find the book by using the signs posted on the bookcases. Discuss how using the library can help you research information for school, career, and home life. Talk about how libraries are funded and how you can help expand the resources and facilities available at your library.

Mock Congress Session

Host a mock Congress session in which the girls represent Congress delegates from different states in the United States of America or countries from the United Nations. Teach the girls the basics of parliamentary procedure and let each girl (or group of girls) write a bill to submit for consideration to the Congress. Then, following parliamentary procedure, let the girls debate the bills and vote on them as in a real session of Congress.

Moral Topics

For this activity, supply your class with a large number of General Conference reports and *Ensign* magazines. Write several topics of moral concern on slips of paper and put them into a hat. Topics could include gambling, chastity, pornography, dress standards, honesty, dating standards, abortion, and the Word of Wisdom, for example. Let each girl draw a few topics out of the hat and then search through Church magazines and conference reports for statements made by General Authorities regarding the position of the Church on their topics. When everyone has finished researching, share what you have learned with each other.

** Helps fulfill a Mia Maid 2 Choice And Accountability Value Experience*

Nutrition Awareness

Ask a nutritionist to come and speak to your girls about the importance of good nutrition during the teenage years, and give the girls specific recommendations for healthy snacks and meals and ideas for eating enough healthy food every day. Ask about the recommendations of national nutrition programs, and compare how well these recommendations parallel the counsel given in the Word of Wisdom (see *Doctrine And Covenants* 89). Talk about the dangers of overeating and eating disorders, and give suggestions for overcoming these challenges.

**Helps fulfill a Mia Maid 2 Choice And Accountability Value Experience and may help fulfill a Beehive 2 Knowledge Value Experience, a Mia Maid 1 Knowledge Value Experience, and a Mia Maid 2 Knowledge Value Experience*

Panning For Gold

After obtaining the proper equipment and finding a

good location, go panning for gold together. Learn how to extract gold from other metals and dirt. Talk about iron pyrite (fool's gold) and how to tell the difference between real gold and its counterfeit.

Personal Progress Trivia

Prior to this activity, search through a Personal Progress book and develop several trivia questions for which the answers are found in the Personal Progress book. For the activity, play a trivia game that requires girls to answer questions about the Personal Progress program. Questions could be anything from, "What color represents the value Faith?" to "Name at least three of the Standards of Personal Worthiness." You might let them bring their Personal Progress books to use if necessary in finding the answers, or you could require that they study their Personal Progress books prior to this activity and give their answers strictly from memory. It might be fun to play this game as a combined Young Women group or along with the parents of the girls.

Political Awareness Night

Ask a qualified person to come and speak to the girls about political issues. Avoid giving personal political opinions, but discuss voter information, facts about current issues, and basic differences between political parties. If possible, bring an actual ballot and discuss what the issues actually mean and the implications of a 'yes' or a 'no' answer.

Product Evaluation

Take the girls to a grocery store and let each of them select a product to evaluate. Each girl should check the number of different brands of the product and the number of sizes, weights, and amounts of the product carried by the store. She should calculate which brand and size is the best buy for the money and list the different types of packages in which the product is available. She should determine which label is, in her opinion, the most appealing to consumers and note which promotional devices the store might be using to sell the item. After this activity, meet back at the church and let the girls report on their findings.

**May help fulfill a Mia Maid 1 Knowledge Value Experience and a Mia Maid 2 Knowledge Value Experience*

Public Health Presentation

Invite a public health worker to come and speak to your girls about the four leading causes of death among people in your country in general, and the four leading causes of death specifically among youth or young women. Give ideas of what the girls can do to avoid these dangers as much as possible. Ask the health worker to discuss any specific health concerns in your community as well.

Recycle It!

Ask someone from your local waste management department to come and speak to the girls about the benefits of recycling and the types of products that should be recycled in your area, or take a tour of your local recycling plant. Show examples of common recyclable containers and examples of products made from recycled materials.

**May help fulfill a Mia Maid 1 Knowledge Value Experience and a Mia Maid 2 Knowledge Value Experience*

Scripture Jeopardy

This activity is a game with rules similar to those for the television game show "Jeopardy." One youth leader is the hostess; she asks players questions phrased as answers, and the players must give the correct answers phrased as questions. For example, in Scripture Jeopardy, the hostess might ask the question, "He gave the golden plates to Joseph Smith on the Hill Cumorah." A player must successfully answer the question with, "Who is Moroni?" Before playing, write several questions from books of scripture and play Scripture Jeopardy with your girls as individuals or as teams.

Seventy Two Hour Kits

Invite the ward food storage specialist, emergency preparedness chairman, or other qualified person to give your class a presentation about 72-hour emergency kits. Be sure that whoever gives this presentation does not try to sell a product during the activity. The presentation should focus on essential items needed for three days of survival, and the presenter should display an actual 72-hour emergency kit and its contents. Discuss the most likely types of emergencies that would occur in your area and how to prepare for them. If the young women or their families already have 72-hour kits, invite the girls to bring them and evaluate their contents as part of this activity.

Sexually Transmitted Disease Awareness

Ask a carefully selected women's doctor to speak to your girls about the dangers of sexually transmitted diseases. Focus on the blessings that come from following the commandment to stay morally clean and pure. This activity works especially well if you can locate a Latter-day Saint doctor who will incorporate Church teachings with medical science in his or her presentation.

**May help fulfill a Mia Maid 2 Choice And Accountability Value Experience*

"Somewhere Out There"

For this marriage preparation night, talk about the process of preparing for and selecting a spouse. Discuss qualities to look for in a future spouse and ways the girls can prepare now for this most important relationship. Remind the girls that "somewhere out there" their mates are preparing for them, and they need to get ready and remain worthy for them. Stress that it is more important to be the right person than to find the right person. You could also show the video clip from the movie *An American Tail* where the mice sing this song to each other.

Summer Job Clinic

Invite an employee from a job placement service to come and speak to the young women about summer job opportunities in your area. Discuss qualifications, income potential, job requirements, and possibilities for promotions within the companies.

Thrift Store Fashion Show

For the first part of this activity, go to a thrift store and let each girl choose and purchase items to create an outfit that she will wear at your Thrift Store Fashion Show. For the second part of this activity, sponsor a fashion show where the girls wear and model the outfits they purchased at the thrift store.

White Elephant Gift Exchange

Each young woman brings a wrapped white elephant gift (a white elephant gift is a gag gift, usually a used item brought from home which she has permission to give away) to this activity. All the girls sit in a circle facing inward and put their gifts in the center of the circle. A leader numbers each gift beginning with #1, and numbers several slips of paper beginning with #1, so that there is one numbered slip of paper for each young woman. Put the slips of paper in a hat and let each girl draw a number. The girl who drew #1 selects a present and unwraps it. She places the gift in front of her so the other girls can see it. Then, the girl who drew #2 can either take #1's gift, leaving #1 to unwrap a new gift, or she can unwrap her own gift from the center of the circle. The girl who drew #3 then can either take #1's or #2's gift or select a wrapped gift from the middle, leaving the girl without a gift to open a new gift. The girl with the highest number will have the greatest advantage, because she will get to choose whichever gift she wants. Continue playing until all the girls have gifts to take home.

> **Variation:** Each girl brings a new, wrapped Christmas ornament that she plans to give away to this activity. Following the same rules for numbering and exchanging gifts, have a Christmas ornament exchange.

chapter six

Good Works

Adopt A Highway

For a long term activity, register your youth group to maintain a section of highway near your neighborhood with the Adopt A Highway Program. This is a great way to clean up the earth and be of service to your community.

** Helps fulfill a Mia Maid 1 Knowledge Value Experience and a Mia Maid 1 Good Works Value Experience and may help fulfill a Beehive 2 Good Works Value Experience and a Mia Maid 2 Good Works Value Experience*

Variation: For a short term activity, clean up any trashy section of highway or other road in your area.

** Helps fulfill a Mia Maid 1 Knowledge Value Experience and a Mia Maid 1 Good Works Value Experience and may help fulfill a Beehive 2 Good Works Value Experience and a Mia Maid 2 Good Works Value Experience*

Art Festival

As a class, organize and sponsor a ward art festival. Invite all ward members to participate by displaying various art exhibits in the cultural hall of your ward building.

Variation: Attend a community-sponsored art festival in your area. They are usually held outdoors in the summer and are often free of charge.

Babysitting Night

Pass out invitations to all parents in your ward with small children, inviting them to bring their children to the ward for a night of free babysitting so they can go on a date or to the temple. Set up a large nursery, bring your babysitting bags, and tend the children for their parents during mutual. Be sure that the children's parents understand what time they must return to pick up their children.

** Helps fulfill a Beehive 1 Good Works Value Experience and a Mia Maid 1 Good Works Value Experience and may help fulfill a Beehive 2 Good Works Value Experience and a Mia Maid 2 Good Works Value Experience*

Variation: Give a break to some of the single parents in your ward by offering this free babysitting service to them.

** Helps fulfill a Beehive 1 Good Works Value Experience and a Mia Maid 1 Good Works Value Experience and may help fulfill a Beehive 2 Good Works Value Experience and a Mia Maid 2 Good Works Value Experience*

Bishop's Storehouse

With the permission of proper priesthood leaders, volunteer your class's services at the bishop's storehouse in your area. You might stock shelves, help fill orders, clean the store or the warehouse, organize paperwork, or help take inventory.

** May help fulfill a Beehive 2 Good Works Value Experience, a Mia Maid 1 Good Works Value Experience, and a Mia Maid 2 Good Works Value Experience*

Car Wash

Offer a free car wash in your neighborhood. Make signs directing cars to your church parking lot where you have set up water, soap, sponges, and towels. Wash the cars free of charge for anyone interested in this service. When each car is finished, give one person in each car a free Church brochure or a *Book of Mormon.*

** Helps fulfill a Mia Maid 1 Good Works Value Experience and may help fulfill a Beehive 2 Good Works Value Experience and a Mia Maid 2 Good Works Value Experience*

Clothing Drive

Coordinate with a local charity to sponsor a clothing drive in your area. Arrange with the charity for its staff to provide the advertising and for the young women to provide the labor. On the appointed day of the drive, organize into groups, establish routes, and drive around your neighborhood to pick up the clothing being donated to the charitable organization. Youth leaders should drive the vehicles while the youth collect the clothing. Deliver the clothing to the charitable organization.

** May help fulfill a Beehive 1 Knowledge Value Experience, a Beehive 2 Knowledge Value Experience, a Beehive 2 Good Works Value Experience, a Mia Maid 1 Knowledge Value Experience, a Mia Maid 1 Good Works Value Experience, and a Mia Maid 2 Good Works Value Experience*

Variation: Hold a canned food drive instead. Collect canned food from families in your neighborhood and donate it to a local charity or soup kitchen. Ask the charity or soup kitchen what types of foods, if any, it will not accept (such as home-canned fruits and vegetables), and be sure to include this information in the pre-collection advertising.

** May help fulfill a Beehive 1 Knowledge Value Experience, a Beehive 2 Knowledge Value Experience, a Beehive 2 Good Works Value Experience, a Mia Maid 1 Knowledge Value Experience, a Mia Maid 1 Good Works Value Experience, and a Mia Maid 2 Good Works Value Experience*

Computer Repair

Invite a computer technician or experienced computer user to come and teach your class how to perform simple computer repairs. He should bring a computer to this activity to show and use. Ask him to show the basic components of a computer and tell why each one is important. He could install a modem, replace or install a hard drive, find and remove a virus, assemble a disconnected computer, or install a driver, for example.

Custodial Services

Contact the Preventative Maintenance group that takes care of your church building and ask what types of custodial work your group might be able to do as a service project for the Church. If there are things that need to be cleaned and the custodians would appreciate your help in cleaning them, you could be of great assistance to the maintenance of your building. Things like washing folding chairs, repairing hymn books, sweeping an outdoor pavilion, cleaning chalkboards and erasers, pulling weeds, and painting church picnic tables are specific suggestions for this activity.

** Helps fulfill a Beehive 1 Good Works Value Experience and may help fulfill a Beehive 2 Good Works Value Experience, a Mia Maid 1 Good Works Value Experience, and a Mia Maid 2 Good Works Value Experience*

Easter Egg Hunt

Plan and provide an Easter egg hunt for the Primary children in your ward. Decorate hard boiled or plastic Easter eggs and hide them all over the outside or inside of your ward building. Invite the Primary children to come and search for the hidden eggs. After all of the eggs are found, sit down with the children and explain the significance of Easter and how it represents the resurrection of the Savior. Talk about how the Easter egg represents "new life." After this activity, inspect your building and collect any Easter eggs that might have been missed by the Primary children.

Envelope Stuffing

Volunteer the services of the young women to stuff envelopes for a local charity or non-profit organization.

** May help fulfill a Beehive 2 Good Works Value Experience, a Mia Maid 1 Good Works Value Experience, and a Mia Maid 2 Good Works Value Experience*

Family Home Evening Clinic

Host a Family Home Evening Clinic in which each girl must come prepared to present at least one idea for a terrific Family Home Evening. Type up the ideas and include any patterns for visual aids or handouts and ideas for refreshments, songs, scriptures, and lessons. Compile all of the ideas into a Family Home Evening Book, and copy the book for each girl to take home and use with her family in the future.

** May help fulfill a Beehive 2 Faith Value Experience, a Beehive*

2 Good Works Value Experience, and a Mia Maid 1 Faith Value Experience

Fire Insurance Video

For this activity, you might want to split your girls into small groups. Each group should obtain a video camera and a blank video and get permission from the parents of at least one of the girls in the group to perform this activity in their home. Upon reaching the home, first let the girls conduct a home fire safety survey, looking for potential fire hazards and warning the family about them. Then, with the video camera, the girls should videotape the house inside and out, filming as many belongings in the home as possible. Give the video to the girl's parents and instruct them to store it in a safe place (such as a fire proof safe) to help them replace lost items in the event of a house fire by having a visual record of what was lost.

** May help fulfill a Beehive 1 Good Works Value Experience, a Beehive 2 Good Works Value Experience, a Mia Maid 1 Good Works Value Experience, and a Mia Maid 2 Good Works Value Experience*

Variation: Instead of going to someone's house for this activity, video your church building inside and out as a service project for your ward. Give the video to your bishop when you are done to keep at his home for safekeeping.

** May help fulfill a Beehive 2 Good Works Value Experience, a Mia Maid 1 Good Works Value Experience, and a Mia Maid 2 Good Works Value Experience*

Variation: Use a camera to take several photographs of the church building and property, inside and out. Develop the film and give the photographs to the bishop when you are done to keep at his home for safekeeping.

** May help fulfill a Beehive 2 Good Works Value Experience, a Mia Maid 1 Good Works Value Experience, and a Mia Maid 2 Good Works Value Experience*

Funeral Flowers

Call a funeral home and ask its management if you could have any extra flowers to use for a service project. Make corsages or other flower arrangements with the fresh flowers and deliver them to elderly people in your area.

** May help fulfill a Beehive 1 Good Works Value Experience, a Beehive 2 Good Works Value Experience, a Mia Maid 1 Good Works Value Experience, and a Mia Maid 2 Good Works Value Experience*

Gardening Helpers

During the spring or summer, ask your bishop for a few names of people in your ward who could use some assistance caring for their gardens. Get the permission of these people and then, for mutual, go to their gardens and help them plant, weed, water, harvest produce, rotor till, or dig furrows.

** May help fulfill a Beehive 1 Good Works Value Experience, a Beehive 2 Good Works Value Experience, a Mia Maid 1 Good Works Value Experience, and a Mia Maid 2 Good Works Value Experience*

Halloween Treat Plates

Sometime during the month of October, begin a Halloween treat plate chain in your neighborhood. Prepare several plates of Halloween goodies and secretly deliver them to people in your area. Include the following with each plate: 1) a note that explains that the treat is from someone who loves them, 2) a picture of a ghost that they must hang on their front door to show that they have been "spooked by the Halloween ghost," and 3) instructions that they must prepare and secretly deliver two treat plates to two additional neighbors within 24 hours. You will be amazed how many people will be "spooked" over the next few weeks as the chain continues through your neighborhood.

High School Cleanup

The property around a high school is often in need of cleanup. Give a trash bag to each of the young women and go to a high school in your neighborhood that needs to have trash removed. Spend the mutual activity cleaning up trash there.

** Helps fulfill a Mia Maid 1 Knowledge Value Experience and a Mia Maid 1 Good Works Value Experience and may help fulfill a Beehive 2 Good Works Value Experience and a Mia Maid 2 Good Works Value Experience*

Home Beautification

For this activity, teach the young women how to make something that would beautify their homes. Some home beautification class ideas: picture framing and picture arranging, wallpaper hanging, flower arranging, sewing tablecloths, and sewing curtains.

** Helps fulfill a Beehive 1 Good Works Value Experience and may help fulfill a Beehive 1 Knowledge Value Experience, a Beehive 2 Good Works Value Experience, a Mia Maid 1 Knowledge Value Experience, and a Mia Maid 2 Knowledge Value Experience*

Hospital Visits

Visit patients in a hospital. Read to them, perform musical numbers for them, do a puppet show for hospitalized children, or just talk to the patients.

** May help fulfill a Beehive 2 Good Works Value Experience, a Mia Maid 1 Good Works Value Experience, and a Mia Maid 2 Good Works Value Experience*

Variation: Make finger puppets for hospitalized children. Perform a puppet show for them with the finger puppets and then give the finger puppets to the children before you leave.

** May help fulfill a Beehive 2 Good Works Value Experience, a Mia Maid 1 Good Works Value Experience, and a Mia Maid 2 Good Works Value Experience*

Variation: Dress up as clowns or pantomimes, learn a simple skit, and then go to the hospital in costumes to perform for hospitalized children. Remember, laughter is sometimes the best medicine.

** May help fulfill a Beehive 2 Good Works Value Experience, a Mia Maid 1 Individual Worth Value Experience, a Mia Maid 1 Good Works Value Experience, a Mia Maid 2 Knowledge Value Experience, and a Mia Maid 2 Good Works Value Experience*

Infant Mobiles

Design and construct infant mobiles out of brightly colored posterboard and yarn to give to the new babies born in your ward. As a class, deliver the mobiles to the mothers and new babies.

** May help fulfill a Beehive 2 Good Works Value Experience, a Mia Maid 1 Good Works Value Experience, and a Mia Maid 2 Good Works Value Experience*

Variation: Make and deliver baby blankets for the babies instead of infant mobiles.

** May help fulfill a Beehive 2 Good Works Value Experience, a*

Mia Maid 1 Good Works Value Experience, and a Mia Maid 2 Good Works Value Experience

Letters For The Disabled

For this activity, visit some disabled ward members who would like assistance writing letters to their families and friends. Take stationery and pens with you and write the letters as they dictate them to you. Put the letters in envelopes, seal them, and address them before you leave. Offer to stamp and mail the letters too, if they need the help.

** May help fulfill a Beehive 2 Good Works Value Experience, a Mia Maid 1 Good Works Value Experience, and a Mia Maid 2 Good Works Value Experience*

Manicure Workshop

For this two part activity, have a manicure workshop the first week where someone comes to your class and teaches the girls how to do professional manicures. For the second week, go with your class to a local retirement center and give manicures to willing residents.

Missionaries And Military Servicemen

Write letters to the missionaries and military servicemen serving from your ward. Thank them for their service and give them words of inspiration and encouragement. Include information regarding the current events within your ward, such as anyone who has gotten married, had a baby, or moved away. Prepare treats to send with the letters and wrap everything in brightly colored packages to mail to the missionaries and servicemen.

New Mother's Helpers

Arrange with a mother of a new baby in your ward to

spend this mutual activity at her home performing acts of service for her. Some ideas of things she might need: wash dishes, fold laundry, wash windows, vacuum, mend clothes, and iron clothes.

** Helps fulfill a Mia Maid 1 Good Works Value Experience and may help fulfill a Beehive 1 Good Works Value Experience, a Beehive 2 Good Works Value Experience, and a Mia Maid 2 Good Works Value Experience*

Old Doll Overhaul

Obtain several used dolls and ask the girls in your class to bring scraps of ribbon, fabric, buttons, needles and thread, and felt. Spend the evening cleaning up the dolls and making new clothes for them. Wash the dolls' hair and bodies, dress them, and fix their hair. When you are finished, donate the dolls either to little girls in your area who would enjoy them or to a local charity.

** Helps fulfill a Mia Maid 1 Good Works Value Experience and may help fulfill a Beehive 2 Good Works Value Experience and a Mia Maid 2 Good Works Value Experience*

Paint A House

If you can get some training and some donated paint for this service project, locate a family in your area who needs its home, barn, or shed painted and would like your class to paint it. Then, after learning basic painting skills and getting proper supplies, carefully paint it for the family.

** Helps fulfill a Mia Maid 1 Good Works Value Experience and may help fulfill a Beehive 1 Good Works Value Experience, a Beehive 2 Good Works Value Experience, and a Mia Maid 2 Good Works Value Experience*

Personal Ancestral File

Talk with your local school district about loading the Personal Ancestral File (PAF) genealogy program onto the computers at a school computer lab. If this is possible, schedule a time for your class to go to the computer lab and learn to use PAF, each young woman on a separate computer. Ask someone familiar with the program to come to this activity, teach the girls how to use the program, answer questions, and talk about the advantages of doing genealogy on a computer.

Quilt Tying

Learn to tie a quilt as a class. Finish the quilt and present it to a needy family, a new mother, or a new bride in your ward.

** Helps fulfill a Mia Maid 1 Good Works Value Experience and may help fulfill a Beehive 1 Good Works Value Experience, a Beehive 2 Good Works Value Experience, a Mia Maid 1 Knowledge Value Experience, a Mia Maid 2 Knowledge Value Experience, and a Mia Maid 2 Good Works Value Experience*

Serve The Bishop Night

Prior to this activity, contact the bishop of your ward and ask him for some specific service projects your class could do for him to show your appreciation for him. Some ideas might be washing and vacuuming his car, cleaning his garage, or doing his yard work.

** Helps fulfill a Mia Maid 1 Good Works Value Experience and may help fulfill a Beehive 1 Good Works Value Experience, a Beehive 2 Good Works Value Experience, and a Mia Maid 2 Good Works Value Experience*

Service Recognition Night

Make certificates of recognition or blue ribbons to present to individuals that serve your community on a regular basis. Then, present the certificates or ribbons to them. If they cannot come to mutual to receive their certificates, deliver or mail them. Some individuals to consider recognizing: firemen, policemen, paramedics, librarians, the mayor, members of the city council, or members of any local volunteer organization.

** Helps fulfill a Beehive 1 Divine Nature Value Experience and may help fulfill a Mia Maid 2 Knowledge Value Experience*

Sock Dolls

Sew sock dolls and give them to the little girls in your ward. A good pattern for sock dolls can be found in *Creative Homemaking For Happy Living: Relief Society Homemaking Booklet* (The Church of Jesus Christ of Latter Day Saints, 1984, pp. 85-86, 94).

** Helps fulfill a Mia Maid 1 Good Works Value Experience and may help fulfill a Beehive 1 Knowledge Value Experience, a Beehive 1 Good Works Value Experience, a Beehive 2 Good Works Value Experience, a Mia Maid 1 Knowledge Value Experience, a Mia Maid 2 Knowledge Value Experience, and a Mia Maid 2 Good Works Value Experience*

Soup Kitchen

Visit your local soup kitchen as a class and help serve a meal to the homeless people who have come there to eat.

** Helps fulfill a Mia Maid 1 Good Works Value Experience and may help fulfill a Beehive 2 Good Works Value Experience and a Mia Maid 2 Good Works Value Experience*

Special Olympics

If the Special Olympics are scheduled to occur in your area, volunteer your class to help administer them. Call your local Special Olympics chapter or other program for the handicapped in your area to schedule a time when your class can be of assistance to the handicapped people by helping them perform some of the Special Olympic events. Some events you may be able to help with: horseback riding, swimming, or bowling.

** Helps fulfill a Mia Maid 1 Good Works Value Experience and may help fulfill a Beehive 2 Divine Nature Value Experience, a Beehive 2 Good Works Value Experience, and a Mia Maid 2 Good Works Value Experience*

Stuffed Animals

Obtain a pattern and supplies for making homemade stuffed animals. Sew the stuffed animals and donate them to organizations where they will be placed in the hands of children in need.

** Helps fulfill a Mia Maid 1 Good Works Value Experience and may help fulfill a Beehive 1 Knowledge Value Experience, a Beehive 2 Good Works Value Experience, a Mia Maid 1 Knowledge Value Experience, a Mia Maid 2 Knowledge Value Experience, and a Mia Maid 2 Good Works Value Experience*

Toilet Paper The Missionaries

Obtain one roll of toilet paper for each missionary serving a full-time mission from your ward. Using magic markers, carefully write letters to the missionaries on the toilet paper by starting on the outermost edge of the roll and writing inward, so that the letters can be read as the toilet paper is unrolled. After you have finished writing the letters, carefully roll the toilet paper back up and send the toilet paper rolls to the missionaries in the mail.

Toys For Nursery

As a class, make toys to donate to the ward nursery closet. You could build and paint wooden blocks, cars, or trains, sew fabric dolls and doll clothes, or draw sewing cards, to name a few examples.

** Helps fulfill a Mia Maid 1 Good Works Value Experience and may help fulfill a Beehive 1 Knowledge Value Experience, a Beehive 2 Good Works Value Experience, and a Mia Maid 2 Good Works Value Experience*

Variation: Make visual aids for the nursery closet. Draw pictures (or cut out pictures from the *Friend* magazine) for the teachers to use in lessons or use them to decorate the nursery classroom. You could also make a flannel board and flannel board pictures of scripture stories for the nursery leaders to file for future use.

** Helps fulfill a Mia Maid 1 Good Works Value Experience and may help fulfill a Beehive 2 Good Works Value Experience and a Mia Maid 2 Good Works Value Experience*

Variation: Clean and sterilize the toys in the Primary nursery closet.

** Helps fulfill a Mia Maid 1 Good Works Value Experience and may help fulfill a Beehive 2 Good Works Value Experience and a Mia Maid 2 Good Works Value Experience*

Tutoring

Set up a free tutoring service for children in your ward who need help with their schoolwork. Invite such children to mutual and assign them to work with young women who can help them in their individual academic needs. Young women could help the children with reading, writing, spelling, arithmetic, science, history, or art, for example.

** Helps fulfill a Mia Maid 1 Good Works Value Experience and may help fulfill a Beehive 1 Divine Nature Value Experience, a Beehive 1 Good Works Value Experience, a Beehive 2 Good Works Value Experience, a Mia Maid 1 Knowledge Value Experience, and a Mia Maid 2 Good Works Value Experience*

Twelve Days of Christmas

Select a less active family in your ward and do the Twelve Days of Christmas for the family. Starting on December 13th, secretly deliver a small gift (i.e. a poem, a Christmas story, a tree ornament, or a Christmas goodie), to the family on each of the twelve days prior to Christmas.

** Helps fulfill a Mia Maid 1 Good Works Value Experience and may help fulfill a Beehive 2 Good Works Value Experience*

Value Flags

As a class, make seven value flags, each flag in one of the seven Young Women Value colors (white, blue, red, green, orange, yellow, and purple), to represent the seven Young Women Values. You could sew seven large fabric squares of the seven value colors and attach them to wooden or metal posts, you could make attractive flags out of heavy laminated construction paper or posterboard, or you could design flags on a computer and print them out on heavy paper. Display the flags in your classroom or other appropriate place in your ward building when you are finished.

** Helps fulfill a Mia Maid 2 Good Works Value Experience and may help fulfill a Mia Maid 1 Integrity Value Experience*

Weeding For The Elderly

As a group, visit elderly ward members and weed their yards for them. Remember to take garbage bags for the weeds with you and remove the bags of weeds when you leave.

** Helps fulfill a Mia Maid 2 Good Works Value Experience and may help fulfill a Beehive 1 Good Works Value Experience, a Beehive 2 Good Works Value Experience, and a Mia Maid 1 Good Works Value Experience*

Welcome Neighbors

Welcome new neighbors moving into your ward boundaries by helping them move in. Under their direction, help clean their house, unload the moving truck, arrange furniture and belongings, or tend their children. In addition, you could deliver a hot meal for them to eat on their first day of living in their new home.

** Helps fulfill a Mia Maid 1 Good Works Value Experience and may help fulfill a Beehive 1 Good Works Value Experience, a Beehive 2 Good Works Value Experience, and a Mia Maid 2 Good Works Value Experience*

Welcome Packets

Make welcome packets to give to new LDS families that move into your ward. In each packet, include a ward phone number list, a city map, neighborhood information such as a list of grocery stores and libraries, a list of ward auxiliary leaders and their phone numbers, a Church meeting schedule, a list of possible babysitters, a "Welcome To Our Ward" sign, and a box of treats. Keep the packets handy so that when new families move into the ward, you can deliver them promptly.

** Helps fulfill a Mia Maid 1 Good Works Value Experience and* *may help fulfill a Beehive 2 Good Works Value Experience and a Mia Maid 2 Good Works Value Experience*

Yard Work

Ask the bishop to identify ward members who could use some help with their yard work. During the spring or fall when yard work is greatest, go to those ward members' homes and do yard work for them. You could dig ditches, make furrows, water plants, or trim rose bushes, for example.

** Helps fulfill a Mia Maid 1 Good Works Value Experience and may help fulfill a Beehive 1 Good Works Value Experience, a Beehive 2 Good Works Value Experience, and a Mia Maid 2 Good Works Value Experience*

Zoo Service Project

With the permission of the manager of your local zoo, volunteer to help feed the animals at the zoo. Before you go, let each girl take a fun quiz, attempting to answer questions about what different animals eat, how much they eat, and how often they are fed. After your class helps feed the zoo animals, let the girls correct their own quizzes to see how much they have learned.

** May help fulfill a Beehive 2 Good Works Value Experience, a Mia Maid 1 Good Works Value Experience, and a Mia Maid 2 Good Works Value Experience*

chapter seven

Integrity

Ancestors With Integrity

Require the girls to come to this activity prepared with stories about their ancestors that show those ancestors acting with integrity. Bring photographs of the ancestors also, if possible. Discuss how living a life of integrity blessed the ancestors' lives as well as the lives of their posterity.

** Helps fulfill a Mia Maid 2 Individual Worth Value Experience*

Angel Making

Paint ceramic angels together. While you are painting, discuss how the Holy Ghost can influence the girls for good if they "don't go where angels fear to tread" and "stand in holy places." Ask each girl to think of a time when she followed a prompting of the Holy Ghost that encouraged her not to go somewhere or participate in a sinful activity. Encourage the girls to share their stories with each other if they desire.

** May help fulfill a Beehive 1 Knowledge Value Experience, a Mia Maid 1 Knowledge Value Experience, and a Mia Maid 2 Knowledge Value Experience*

Babysitting Bags

Make babysitting bags. Include storybooks, crayons, coloring books, a flannel board and flannel board figures, craft ideas, a recipe for homemade play dough and finger paints, and other educational activities for children. Include a book with first aid information, parents' profiles, important phone numbers, child care tips, and a list of questions to ask parents before they leave on an outing.

Bishop's Survey

Prior to this activity, a Young Women leader should contact the bishop and ask him to name the top five sins which he believes challenge today's young people. Then, plan a mutual activity which addresses these sins and gives the young women ideas for resisting them. Give the bishop the opportunity to speak to the girls on these subjects as part of this activity.

Career Conduct

Discuss with the girls what kind of conduct is appropriate when working as an employee. Talk about job ethics and proper manners and answer job-related questions such as how to treat your boss, how to ask for a raise, how to ask for time off, what to do if you will be late for work, and how important it is to always do your best on the job.

Code of Honor

As a class, write a code of honor together and promise each other to live by it. Make a copy for everyone in the class and memorize it.

** May help fulfill a Mia Maid 1 Integrity Value Experience*

Variation: Use 1 Corinthians 3:16 as the basis for your code of honor. Discuss the importance of keeping your bodies healthy and free from dangers like drugs and alcohol. Promise each other to live by the code of honor that you write together. If you desire, you might want to have a health professional come to part of this activity and speak to your girls about the dangers of drugs and alcohol prior to writing this code of honor.

** Helps fulfill a Beehive 2 Knowledge Value Experience and may help fulfill a Mia Maid 2 Choice And Accountability Value Experience*

Employment 101

Host an evening where the girls in your class learn techniques for getting and keeping a job. Focus on such issues as: writing a letter of application, writing a formal resume, making telephone contact, going in for an interview, following up with potential employers, following proper ethics while on the job, and obtaining letters of recommendation.

Flowers In The City

With the permission of your city council, locate an area of public property that needs beautification. For the activity, weed the area, plant flowers (or flower seeds), water the soil, fertilize or trim shrubs, remove trash, and make the area look as nice as possible. If possible, attend to the area on a regular basis to keep it looking attractive.

** Helps fulfill a Mia Maid 1 Knowledge Value Experience and a Mia Maid 1 Good Works Value Experience and may help fulfill a Beehive 2 Good Works Value Experience and a Mia Maid 2 Good Works Value Experience*

Graffiti No More

Locate an area in your city that has been vandalized with graffiti, and with the proper permission, clean off the graffiti for a mutual activity. You will either need to remove the graffiti or paint over it. If you must remove it, remember that it is a tough job, dress appropriately, and come prepared with good cleaning agents. If you must paint over it, get some donated paint, learn proper painting techniques, and carefully paint the area. Make sure to schedule this activity during the day while it is still light outside.

** Helps fulfill a Mia Maid 1 Knowledge Value Experience and a Mia Maid 1 Good Works Value Experience and may help fulfill a Beehive 2 Good Works Value Experience and a Mia Maid 2 Good Works Value Experience*

Integrity Panel Discussion

Invite three socially mature women to sit on a panel and discuss with your class issues such as how to cultivate good manners, how to apologize, how to say "thank you," how to offer to help, how to put another person at ease, what to do in an embarrassing situation, and how to accept a compliment.

** May help fulfill a Mia Maid 2 Integrity Value Experience*

Variation: Host a panel discussion of young men and young women to discuss ways that LDS teenagers can be positive influences on their friends.

** May help fulfill a Mia Maid 2 Integrity Value Experience*

Internet Awareness

This activity may take two consecutive mutual nights to complete. Hold the first part of this activity at the home of a proficient Internet user. Invite her to demonstrate how to use the Internet and how to find desired information on the web. Ask her to define and discuss common Internet terms such as: web site, web page, home page, search engine, surfing, chat rooms, servers, logging on, and logging off. Then, for the second part of this activity, return to the church building and hold a discussion led by an adult youth leader or bishopric member about the potential dangers of the Internet. Recommend ways the girls can protect themselves from seeing inappropriate material and spending excessive time on the web.

Juvenile Court

Visit juvenile court together as a class. Listen to specific cases of alleged juvenile offenders and then return to the church building to discuss the importance of "obeying, honoring, and sustaining the law." (*Article of Faith* #12)

Let Your Light Shine

Using scriptures that talk about the light of Christ as the basis for this activity, arrange for speakers to come and speak to the girls about the light of Christ and about letting their light shine. Talk about the importance of being good examples, of acting like true followers of the Savior, and of teaching others about the Gospel. Decorate with light bulbs or lanterns.

** May help fulfill a Mia Maid 1 Good Works Value Experience*

Media-Free Challenge

This is a week-long activity which should begin on one mutual night and end on the next. On the first night, lead a discussion about the dangers of inappropriate media, including television, radio, books, magazines, and videotapes. Talk about why Latter-day Saints have been counseled to avoid media which offends the Spirit and wastes time. If possible, provide and read quotes from Latter-day prophets regarding this subject. Then, challenge the young women to go for an entire week without reading, listening to, or viewing any media whatsoever. You may need to provide an incentive such as a class party for those who successfully complete the challenge. Give the girls plenty of ideas of things they can do instead of watching television and listening to music, especially encouraging them to be active and give service. On the second mutual night, let the girls report about their experience.

**May help fulfill a Mia Maid 1 Choice And Accountability Value Experience and a Mia Maid 2 Integrity Value Experience*

Money Management

Invite a banker or other financial manager to come and speak to the girls about preparing financially for the future. Topics covered could include establishing credit, the importance of a good credit rating, the pros and cons of credit cards, balancing a checking account, applying for a car loan, buying a car, investing money, or saving for college.

**May help fulfill a Mia Maid 1 Knowledge Value Experience and a Mia Maid 2 Knowledge Value Experience*

Music Awareness

Often, young women listen to music that contains inappropriate lyrics, yet the girls are unaware of them. Ask the girls to bring their CDs and cassette tapes to this activity. After reminding the girls that inappropriate music offends the Holy Ghost and is spiritually dangerous, locate and read the lyrics of their music together using the album inserts or the Internet, and help them determine which music should be eliminated from their collections.

Primary Videos

Write short skits which teach values to Primary age children. Get costumes and props and videotape your class members acting out the skits. Give the videos to a member of the Primary presidency for use in Sharing Time.

** May help fulfill a Beehive 1 Good Works Value Experience, a Beehive 2 Good Works Value Experience, a Mia Maid 1 Individual Worth Value Experience, a Mia Maid 1 Good Works Value Experience, a Mia Maid 2 Knowledge Value Experience, and a Mia Maid 2 Good Works Value Experience*

Seminary Devotionals

As a class, brainstorm together to come up with seven complete seminary devotionals, one devotional about each of the seven Young Women Values. Type the devotionals on paper to file for future use in seminary.

State Capitol Visit

Visit the State Capitol together and learn about the laws of the city, state, and nation. Take a tour of the building. Discuss the role that the state government plays in the nation, and have someone there speak to the girls about freedom: cherishing it and protecting it. Discuss how laws make us free.

Titles of Liberty

Make titles of liberty together, using Alma 46:12 as your guide. Remind the girls that the purpose of a title of liberty is to commit themselves to a specific cause of righteousness in order to benefit themselves and others whom they love. Provide one T-shirt for each title of liberty and either let each girl make her own or have all the girls work together to make one to share. To make a title of liberty, tear the T-shirt and write a message on it using permanent markers or paints. A modern day example of a title of liberty might be, "In memory of my future spouse and children, I will keep my mind unpolluted by not viewing R-rated or vulgar movies or listening to music which offends the Holy Ghost."

Tree Planting

For this activity, locate an area where your group would be allowed to plant trees. Consider planting trees at your ward meetinghouse or stake center, near a river, in a forest, or even on a friend's private property. Go there with several tree seedlings and plant trees together. Consider planting trees representing the seven Young Women Value colors. For example, faith (white) could be a Spring Snow Crab, divine nature (blue) could be a Blue Spruce, individual worth (red) could be a Scarlet Hawthorne, knowledge (green) could be a Spartan Juniper, choice and accountability (orange) could be a Mountain Ash, good works (yellow) could be a Golden Chain, and integrity (purple) could be a Newport Plum. Call the area your Young Women Value Grove. Make sure that people and facilities are available to care for and protect the seedlings after you leave.

Wall Hangings

As a class, make wall hangings that display either the Young Women Theme, the Young Women Motto, or your Young Women Class Theme. Encourage each girl to take her wall hanging home and arrange with her parents to hang it on a wall where she will see it often.

** Helps fulfill a Beehive 1 Integrity Value Experience and a Mia Maid 1 Integrity Value Experience and may help fulfill a Beehive 1 Knowledge Value Experience, a Beehive 1 Good Works Value Experience, a Mia Maid 1 Knowledge Value Experience, and a Mia Maid 2 Knowledge Value Experience*

Writing A Resume

Give each girl a pencil and a piece of paper and help her draft a resume for herself. Teach the girls what types of things are usually included in resumes and help each girl think of things about herself that would be appropriate for her to include in her own resume. Provide several types of resumes to use as examples. Remember to include the following in each resume: personal information, employment objectives, education, work experience, accomplishments, and references. If time permits, locate a computer or typewriter and let the girls type their resumes for future use.

chapter eight

Combined Activities

Advertising Agents

Divide the young men and young women into mixed teams of 3-4 people each. Place several household items or products on a table such as hair spray, a wire whisk, and toilet paper. There needs to be at least as many items as there are teams. Randomly assign each team a product. Allow twenty to thirty minutes for the groups to create advertisements to sell their products. The advertisements can be dialogues, skits, songs, poems, or a combination of these. Each product should be advertised as something that it is not; for example, a flyswatter can be renamed a "flowip" and can be advertised as a product which flips pancakes. When the time for planning has expired, each team should present its product advertisement to the other teams. Evaluate the effectiveness of the advertisement's influence upon you to buy the product and possibly give awards to the teams such as, "Most Influential Advertisement," "Funniest Advertisement," "Most Creative Advertisement," or "Best Acting."

Alphabet Scavenger Hunt

Divide your group of youth into teams of about three or four people per team. Give each team a piece of paper with all of the letters of the alphabet listed A - Z vertically down the paper. Make sure at least one member of each team has a pen or pencil. At the "go" signal, let each group go on a scavenger hunt for a specific amount of time (approximately 45 minutes) to various homes in your neighborhood, attempting to get an item that begins with each letter of the alphabet (26 total items by the end of the time period). A member of the team writes the name of each item down on its list next to the letter of the alphabet with which the item starts. Another team member carries all of the items procured in a large bag or box. A team can only get one item from each home it visits, and teammates must stay together throughout the hunt. When time is up, all teams must return to the church and show each other the items they have collected. Give a prize to the team that has the most eligible items at the end of the hunt.

Barter For Bigger Or Better

Divide your group of youth into teams of about three or four people on each team. Give each team a small, monetarily worthless object such as a pebble or a dried pinto bean. The teams race against each other to barter for something either bigger in size or better in monetary value than the object with which they start. At the "go" signal, each team must leave the church building and go on a scavenger hunt in search of strangers willing take the team's object and trade it for something either bigger or better. Teams may only trade one time with one person, but may make as many trades with as many different people as they can in a designated time period (about 45 minutes). When time is up, all teams must return to the church with their items to see what everyone ended up with. Award two prizes to two different teams, one to the team with the biggest object and one to the team with thc best object.

Bingo!

This is a variation to the classic game of "Bingo" that will help your youth get to know each other better and appreciate the individual talents and abilities of each person. To begin, give each person a homemade Bingo card with a grid of about a dozen large, blank squares on it. Make sure each player has a pencil with which to write. For the first part of the evening, let everyone mingle around the room, talking with each other and exchanging personal information. They write the name of each person they learn about in one of the squares on their cards and two things about that person such as her talents, family information, favorite food, or hobbies. After everyone has every square on his card filled, ask all the players to sit down and give them several square pieces of construction paper to use as Bingo chips. Write the names of the participants on several slips of paper and put them in a hat. Draw one name out of the hat and read the name aloud. If anyone has that name on her Bingo card, she puts a Bingo chip over that name. Continue reading names and letting the players cover up the names on their cards until at least one person covers an entire row of names (horizontally, vertically, or diagonally). She yells "Bingo!" and reads the names and facts about each person in her Bingo line. Continue playing, giving several players a chance to get Bingo and read about the people on their cards. You can play regular Bingo, double Bingo (requires a participant to cover two complete rows), or blackout Bingo (requires a participant to cover her entire card).

Bopper

This is a good game to play with people who don't know each other very well. Begin by choosing someone to be "it." All players sit in a circle and whoever is "it" stands in the middle of the circle. "It" holds a rolled up newspaper in his hand and calls out the name of someone sitting in the circle. He tries to bop her with the newspaper before she calls out someone else's name. If she calls out another name before being bopped, then "it" must attempt to bop the new person, who also yells out another name, and so on. If he bops her in time, however, then he gives her the newspaper and she becomes "it." Be sure not to bop too hard.

Cat And Mouse

The youth need to bring their scriptures to this activity. Divide everyone into teams of 4-5 people and play one of two ways: 1) The youth leader asks a question from the scriptures and the first team to give the correct answer scores one point, or 2) the youth leader calls out a scripture reference and the first team to have three people locate the reference in their scriptures scores a point.

After choosing which method to use and playing one round, the team who scored the point sends a person to the front of the room. This person is the "cat." The other teams each send two people to the front. These are the "mice." The cat is given the lid of a large pan or pot as his pouncing tool. Each mouse is given a string or light chain with a large paper clip tied to the end of it. The cat and mice then kneel around a circle on the floor that has been made with masking tape. A smaller square also made of tape in the middle of the circle represents a hunk of cheese.

The mice place their paper clips on the piece of cheese and the cat rolls a pair of dice once to determine his pouncing number. Then, the cat begins rolling the dice, attempting to roll his pouncing number or doubles. When he does, he immediately slams down the lid over the cheese, trying to catch the mice. The mice attempt to pull out of the circle before they get caught. Each mouse that escapes scores one point for her team, and the cat gets one point for each mouse that he catches. The cat can "fake pounce" on the wrong number, trying to get the mice to pull out early. If a mouse pulls out of the circle early, he loses one point and the cat gains one point. If a mouse pulls partially out early but stays within the circle, he is still in the game. If the cat fake pounces and the lid accidentally hits the floor, he loses one point for each mouse still in the game and each of those mice score one point. After the cat has pounced, all participants return to their teams and prepare for the next scripture question.

Crazy Olympics

Turn the cultural hall of your ward meetinghouse into an Olympic arena, where teams will come to compete for gold, silver, and bronze medals in comical events. After a short "opening ceremony," allow the athletes to compete in various events such as:

1. The Potato Dash: With pieces of masking tape, mark off 25 feet from start to finish. A contestant must race to the finish line while rolling a potato with a spoon, and the spoon must be held between the contestant's toes.
2. Twenty Foot Dash: Mark off 20 feet from start to finish. Each contestant must race to the finish line while blowing a Styrofoam cup along the floor with his mouth.

3. Hot Air Balloon Race: Give each contestant five balloons. They must blow the balloons up until they pop. The first contestant that successfully pops all five balloons by blowing them wins.
4. The High Jump: Hang glazed doughnut holes from the ceiling by strings, all at the same level. Each athlete must jump up and pull the doughnut hole off of the string using only his mouth. If he succeeds, tie another doughnut hole on the end of the string and raise the string one inch for his next jump. Whoever jumps the highest and successfully bites a doughnut hole off the string wins.
5. Basketball Shoot: Obtain a preschool size soft basketball and basketball stand. Set up the stand 12 feet away from the starting line. A participant must kneel on her knees and attempt to make a basket. Whoever scores the most baskets wins.
6. Speed Skating: Obtain two shoe boxes for each contestant. Contestants must place their feet inside the boxes and wear them as skates. They then line up at a starting line and at the go signal, they skate across the floor to a finish line.

Dating Panel

For this combined activity, invite several young adults with dating experience and strong spiritual values to come and participate in a dating panel for your youth. The people on the panel sit behind a table in front of the youth and answer questions about dating. The youth should each be prepared with two or three specific questions about dating that they would like to ask, and they can either ask them randomly by raising their hands or they can write their questions down on slips of paper and a mediator can draw the questions one at a time and read them aloud. A youth should indicate which panel member he is addressing when he asks his question, although all panel members should be free to make comments and additions to the others' answers. The focus of the activity should be on the benefits of dating, the importance of following Church counsel regarding dating standards, and how youth can prepare now to date after they turn 16 years old.

Day At The Races

Host an activity where the young men and young women must engage in a variety of fun races set up in the cultural hall of your ward meetinghouse. Races may include:

1. Blow a ping pong ball across the floor
2. Push a penny across the floor with your nose
3. Carry a balloon on two yard sticks
4. Crab walk
5. Wheelbarrow race
6. Human wheelbarrow race
7. Roll a glass soda pop bottle across the floor with a stick
8. Do backwards somersaults across the floor
9. Gunny sack race
10. Body roll race

Downtown Foot Rally

Set up a race through your neighborhood that the youth will be able to do on foot and within a one hour time frame. Divide into groups of about four youth per group and give each group a list of questions that they must answer during the race. Questions might be:

1. How many stickers are there in the window of the paint store?

2. What is the highest mailbox number in the post office?
3. How many pumps does the gas station have?
4. What is the most popular video rented this year, according to the video store?
5. How much does it cost to rent a bicycle at the sporting goods store?

At the "go" signal, the groups must walk around town, finding answers to the questions on their lists. Groups must stay together for the entire race. When time is up, everyone returns to the church and determines which group found the most answers to the questions on the lists.

Dress Up Relay

Fill two large boxes with equal amounts of gloves, hats, socks, shoes, scarves, coats, sunglasses, and other paraphernalia (thrift store goodies). Make about three separate lists of the items in each box, each list with the same items but with those items listed in a different order. Divide your group into two or more even teams. Assign a judge from your team to watch the opposing team and provide that team with one of the lists of items in the box. Blindfold one person from each team. On the "go" signal, each blindfolded person approaches his box and his teammates yell out the first item he is to locate and put on. When he has put that item on, his teammates yell to him the second item to put on, and so forth. The blindfolded opponents race to get all of the items on, one by one. When one finishes putting on all of the items on the list, he removes his blindfold and the items and returns the items to the box. He rushes his blindfold to the next person on his team. This next person must blindfold herself and approach the box while the judge gives a new list of items to her teammates. The teammates yell to her which items she must put on and in which order, as before. Continue playing, rotating lists and teammates, until everyone on one team has finished. That team wins.

First Aid Tournament

Prior to this activity, assign each class to prepare to teach a few first aid procedures to the other youth. For the activity, let the class members take turns teaching the others the correct way to perform the procedures. Then, hold a first aid tournament. Set up a first aid procedure at each of several tables, with appropriate supplies available for the youths' use and a youth leader at every table to verify that the procedures are performed correctly. At the "go" signal, race guys against girls to see who is faster at correctly administering the first aid procedures to dolls or stuffed animals.

Flour Power

Tightly pack some white flour into a cup. Carefully turn the cup-shaped block of flour out onto a plate. Set a nickel on top of the flour on its edge. Using a butter knife, take turns cutting slices of the flour apart from the block of flour until someone makes the nickel fall. Whoever makes it fall has to retrieve it with his lips.

Gospel Charades

Divide your youth into two equal teams and play Gospel Charades together. Have a leader write several Gospel-related words on slips of paper and put them all into a hat. One player from the first team draws out a slip of paper and must act out whatever the paper says, so that his teammates can guess what is written on his piece of paper within one minute. He cannot make any noise or write anything down while he is acting. If his teammates guess correctly, his team scores one point. If not, no points are scored. Then, play passes to the next team. Play until everyone has had at least one chance to act for his team. Make time adjustments as necessary if one minute seems too long or short.

Halloween Carnival For Children

Sponsor a Halloween carnival for the Primary children in your ward. Each youth class should prepare and manage one carnival booth. Some Halloween booth ideas are: fish pond, Halloween bingo, bob for apples, carve pumpkins, cake walk, penny toss, bean bag toss, and musical chairs with Halloween music. Invite the children to come in costumes and enjoy the activities you have prepared. Remember that both decorations and costumes must not include masks, demons, blood and gore, or anything else that might be scary or inappropriate.

Heart Attack!

For the first part of this activity, prepare several plates of cookies or other treats and cut out several hearts from construction paper. Get a list of less active families in your ward and their addresses from your bishop. On some of the hearts, write notes to the less active families in your ward such as, "We miss you!" and "Please join us for mutual next week!"and tape those notes to the treat plates. Load the treat plates and the youth into cars and go "heart attacking." Sneak up to the door of one of the families, set that family's plate of goodies on the doorstep, and scatter hearts all over the family's yard. Ring the doorbell, run to the car, and drive to the next house on your list, trying not to be seen by the family. Heart attack every house on your list.

** May help fulfill a Beehive 2 Good Works Value Experience*

Homeless Pets

Before this activity, call your local animal shelter and get permission from an employee to provide this service project for the homeless animals that live at the shelter. For mutual, take your youth to the animal shelter and under the direction of an employee, wash the animals and clean the animal pens. Then, leash some of the animals and take them for a walk outside around the facility.

** May help fulfill a Beehive 2 Good Works Value Experience, a Mia Maid 1 Good Works Value Experience, and a Mia Maid 2 Good Works Value Experience*

Impromptu Skits

Divide the young men and young women into groups. Give each group a large bag full of props which participants must use in a skit which they will write and perform. Members of each group should look through their bag to see what props they must use, and then they must write a skit together using all of the group members and all of the props. Groups draw straws to determine the performance order and then perform their skits for each other.

** May help fulfill a Mia Maid 1 Individual Worth Value Experience and a Mia Maid 2 Knowledge Value Experience*

King of The Mountain

The youth should bring their scriptures to this activity. Arrange several chairs in spiral fashion, winding inward from a wide outer shell to a tight inner circle (from a bird's-eye view, this arrangement looks like a walkway that circles up and around a hill to the very top). The chairs should alternate the direction they face, one forward, one backward, so that the youth sit knee to knee in pairs with their scriptures in their laps, and the person each player faces is his opponent. The youth in the uppermost chair is the King or Queen of the mountain. To play, a youth leader calls out a scripture reference and the students race to find it. The first person in each pair to find it yells, "Got it!" and gently slaps the knee of her opponent. Half of the youth will have won that round and half will have lost. Those who have lost move back one set of chairs to the lower of the two chairs, and those who have won move up one set of chairs to the higher of the two chairs. The object of the game is to see who can hold the highest chair of all (the king's throne) for the longest period of time.

Variation: To play this game with points, give one point per round to the King or Queen who successfully retains the throne. If your group consists of an approximately equal number of young men and young women, let the Kings compete against the Queens by seeing which gender scores the most points.

Love Baskets

Put together several baskets of food and Christmas goodies to deliver to families in your ward shortly before Thanksgiving or Christmas. For a list of families who would especially benefit from this service, contact your bishop prior to the activity. After assembling the baskets, divide your youth into groups, pile into several vehicles, and drive to the families' homes to deliver the love baskets to them. If you are doing this activity shortly before Christmas, sing Christmas carols on the doorstep when the families answer their doors.

** Helps fulfill a Mia Maid 1 Good Works Value Experience and may help fulfill a Beehive 1 Good Works Value Experience, a*

Beehive 2 Good Works Value Experience, and a Mia Maid 2 Good Works Value Experience

Miniature Missions

For this activity, require that everyone come in Sunday dress. As the youth enter the chapel, give them pretend "mission calls" which call them to any of the various missions in the world. Begin in the chapel where your Young Men President pretends he is the Mission President and welcomes the new "missionaries" to their missions. He divides the missionaries (boys with boys, girls with girls) into pairs and requires that the pairs remain together for the duration of the activity. He then directs the missionaries to another part of the church building where they will participate in a variety of missionary activities such as: 1) attend a five minute class where a returned missionary teaches them about the Church in the country where he served, 2) go to the ward kitchen and practice washing at least three dirty dishes, 3) attend a class where your local full-time missionaries give them an overview of the Church missionary discussions, 4) enter a room where they are required to memorize a verse of scripture in a foreign language in order to leave, 5) practice knocking on a closed door and giving an "investigator" (a youth leader) a proper introduction and door approach, and 6) write a letter to his or her parents on "P-day." At the end of the activity, everyone should meet back in the chapel where the "Mission President" releases the youth from their "missions" and talks about the importance of missionary work in the Church.

Missionary Survival

Learn missionary survival skills in a fun way. Set up booths or tables in your ward meetinghouse that help teach missionary survival skills, such as: hemming a pant leg, ironing a tie, washing socks in a sink or basin, preparing a simple meal, or setting a table. Then, divide the youth into pairs or small groups and race to see which "companionship" or "zone" successfully completes each skill in the fastest time. Give awards for the fastest time, the most careful, the most creative, and the best missionary attitudes.

Mock Prom Night

Have the girls and guys come to this activity dressed in formal attire (i.e. whatever they might wear to a high school prom). Spend the evening teaching them proper etiquette and how to behave in a formal setting. You might teach eating manners, common courtesies, how to act like a gentleman or a lady, and dance tips. For a more realistic approach, serve a dinner and let them practice eating and dancing appropriately.

Mock Trial

Prior to this activity, leaders should write a case in which a defendant is to be tried for an alleged wrongdoing. Be sure that the alleged wrongdoing is not too distasteful or improper for the youth to discuss. For the activity, host a mock trial in which the youth play different roles and act out the case as it is presented in a pretend court of law. Some of the youth should be prosecutors, some should be defense lawyers, some should be jury members, one should be a judge, and at least one should be a defendant. Give them time to read the case and plan their parts, and then let the case begin. Follow the proceedings of a regular court session as much as possible and after the jury has presented its verdict, discuss the importance of law and order in a society, and the necessity of being honest and true in one's life.

Mop Hockey

Set up a goal on each side of the cultural hall of your ward building. Make sure every participating youth has a sponge mop. Divide into two equal teams and play mop hockey, using either a tennis ball, a racquetball, or a baseball for the puck and the mops for the hockey sticks. (Note: if your cultural hall has a carpeted floor, you might want to put tape on the mop heads to allow them to slide along the carpet more easily. Be careful not to rip the sponge on your mop head while putting the tape on or while removing it.)

> **Variation:** Play broom hockey instead of mop hockey. Be careful not to swing the brooms too high.

Name That Hymn

For this game, you will need the assistance of someone who plays the piano well. He should sit at a piano with a *Hymns* book. Divide your youth into two teams. Select a player from each team to sit in a chair in the front of the room, facing the group but facing away from the piano. They compete to see who can "name that hymn" in the least amount of piano notes. The first player says, "I can name that hymn in __ notes." The second player either says, "I can name that hymn in __ notes" (less than player 1) or, "Name that hymn" if he doesn't think he can name the hymn in less notes than the first player. The pianist then begins playing a hymn, stopping after the specified number of notes. If the player gets it right, his team gets a point. If not, the other team can steal the point by naming the hymn.

Continue playing as long as you wish, giving an award to the team who scores the most points.

Outdoor Cooking

Sponsor an outdoor cooking event. Divide your group into teams and either assign each team the same recipe to prepare or assign each team to prepare a different part of a meal. The youth could barbecue meats over a grill, cook any number of items in a Dutch oven, or cook something over a campfire. When the food is ready, eat it together.

**May help fulfill a Mia Maid 1 Knowledge Value Experience and a Mia Maid 2 Knowledge Value Experience*

Outdoor Movie

Pick a good movie, pop some popcorn, and set up an outdoor movie screen (either a big screen television or a 16 millimeter film projected onto a pull down screen) in a safe location and in good weather. Watch the movie together.

Parenthood Olympics

Split your youth into two teams: future fathers and future mothers. The teams compete in the Parenthood Olympics, which are Olympic events testing skills in a variety of parental responsibilities. For example, youth could change diapers, wash dishes, put the proper amount of air in a tire, prepare a baby bottle, fold laundry, sew on a button, dress a doll, hammer five nails into a board, or shovel a sidewalk. Keep score and give small awards to the team that demonstrates the highest level of proficiency at performing the parenting chores.

Picnic Party Surprise

Each youth brings one complete meal which he or she has prepared and put on a plate. Place all of the plates of food on a table and give each meal a number. Each person then draws a number out of a hat and takes the meal that corresponds to his number. After everyone has a plate of food (make sure no one gets the plate he prepared himself), eat together around a table.

Quilting Competition

Set up two quilts on quilting frames that need to be tied, one for the young women to tie and one for the young men to tie. Have a race between the young women and young men to see who can tie their quilt the best and the fastest. Donate the finished quilts to charity.

Red Flag Blue Flag

For this game, each participant ties a red and a blue bandana together and the group divides into two teams. Instruct the participants to tuck their flags into their own back pockets with the blue bandana hanging out if they are on the blue team and the red bandanna hanging out if they are on the red team. Everyone sneaks around in the bushes trying to steal each other's flag. When a person is caught, he must join the other team by switching the color of his bandana and hunting members of his former team. The game is over when everyone is on the same color team. If it is difficult for you to obtain enough bandannas to play this game, use any two solid-colored fabric squares instead of bandannas.

Reverse Devotionals

For this activity, the young women must create a seminary devotional about the Scout Oath, and the young men must create a seminary devotional about the Young Women Values. Then, race to see who can memorize the other's oath / theme first: the boys have to memorize the Young Women Theme, and the girls have to memorize the Scout Oath. Give a prize to the winning team.

Rotating Board Games

Set up several tables in a large room of your ward meetinghouse. On each table, set up a board game for at least four players. Divide your youth into groups of about four people per group, and sit each group down at one of the tables. Let each group play the game at its table until you sound a buzzer, signaling that everyone must leave the game exactly as it is and rotate one table to the right. Participants must sit down at the new table and begin playing where the last group left off. Rotate on a regular basis.

Rotating Cards

Set up four or five card tables with card games on them that are familiar to your youth. Some ideas for card games that work well for this activity are: Rook, Uno, Phase 10, and Skip Bo. Divide your youth into even-numbered groups and sit each group down at one of the card tables. Instruct everyone to begin playing the card game at that table. After about eight minutes blow a whistle, upon which all players lay down their cards and rotate to the next table, picking up in the game where the others left off. Rotate on a regular basis.

Scriptionary

Prior to playing this scripture-related version of the game "Pictionary," make several index cards containing words that are specific to the Church such as "liahona," "Blazer," and "Relief Society." Divide a chalkboard in half by drawing a vertical line down the center of it. Provide some chalk and chairs for everyone to sit in. Divide your group of youth into two teams. The first player of each team comes to the chalkboard and one of them selects a card listing an object which both players will attempt to draw for their teams. At the "go" signal, both players draw the object at the same time on the chalkboard, and their teammates attempt to guess what they are drawing. The first team to successfully identify its picture wins a point. Continue playing with new cards and new players in this manner for as long as you desire.

> **Variation:** Play Fingerpaint Scriptionary. Rather than a chalkboard and chalk, use large pieces of butcher paper and Fingerpaints to draw your objects. Cover the floor and tables with newspapers to protect them from damage.

Scripture And Object Hunt

Divide your group of youth into teams of 4-5 people each. A youth leader asks a question to the teams from the scriptures such as, "What does the word Deseret mean?" (See Ether 2:3 for the answer). The first team to answer correctly scores one point. Then, the leader yells out an object which a teenager might have in his possession (such as a shoe lace, a driver's license, or a stick of gum). The first person to bring the correct object to the leader scores a bonus point for his team. After the leader awards the bonus point, he asks another scriptural question to the teams. Play continues in this fashion, with scriptural question first, bonus object question second.

Scripture Battleship

Divide a large room into two equal halves. Tie a rope to volleyball standards and hang several sheets or blankets from the rope to the floor to divide the room and make it so that people on one side of the sheets cannot see the people on the other side. Divide the youth into two teams and have each team get into a strategic position on either side of the divider. Each person represents a military ship. Some should lay down and some should sit up, so that some ships are bigger targets than others. No ships can move around once they are positioned. A youth leader begins the game by asking a question from the scriptures and the person who first answers the question correctly scores an opportunity to shoot five "missiles" (tennis balls) at the opposing team. The person who answered the question correctly can shoot all five missiles himself, or he can give other members of his team a chance to throw some of them. He should throw the tennis ball over the top of the sheets onto the other side, hoping to hit one of the ships positioned on the enemy side. When hit, a ship is sunk and must sit out for the rest of the game. Play continues until one team sinks five enemy ships, and that team wins. (No one can answer two questions in a row.) Play as many rounds as you desire.

Scripture Character Charades

In preparation for this activity, write the names of many well-known scriptural characters on slips of paper and put them in a hat. Divide the young men and young women into two teams and assign a youth leader to act as scorekeeper. A player from team "A" must draw a slip of paper out of the hat and act out the character for his own team while team "B" times him. If team "A" guesses the character within 15 seconds, the team scores 4 points; within 30 seconds = 3 points; within 45 seconds = 2 points; and within 60 seconds = 1 point. If team "A" does not guess the character within 60 seconds, then it scores no points and team "B" gets the opportunity to guess it. If team "B" guesses correctly, it scores two points. Then, a player from team "B" must draw a slip of paper out of the hat and act out a character for his team, as team "A" did before. Alternate turns between teams "A" and "B."

> **Variation:** One player from each team looks at the character on the slip of paper at the same time and then each acts out the character in front of her own team. Whichever team guesses the character first scores a point.

Service Scavenger Hunt

Prepare a scavenger hunt that requires groups of youth to go out into the neighborhood and perform services for willing families. Divide your youth into groups of about four people per group and give each group a list of possible services to perform such as: wash a window, sweep a floor, dust a room, change a diaper, or read a bedtime story. On the "go" signal, youth groups must go from house to house in your neighborhood and ask permission to perform one of the services on its list for the family members in that house. When the group has completed a service, it must have one of the family members sign the list next to the service rendered, verifying that the service was completed to the family's satisfaction. Groups can perform only one service per household and must stay together for the entire activity. After a given amount of time (about 45 minutes), all groups return to the ward meetinghouse to share stories about the activity and see who has completed the most services. If you desire, you may award a small prize to members of the winning group.

** May help fulfill a Beehive 2 Good Works Value Experience, a Mia Maid 1 Good Works Value Experience, and a Mia Maid 2 Good Works Value Experience*

Signature Scavenger Hunt

Divide the youth into teams of about four people per team and give each team a list of categories and a pencil. Teams must go from house to house searching for people who match the categories listed on their papers and have those people sign their names next to one category to which they belong. Teams can get only one signature from any given household and must return to the church building at a certain time, finished or not. Give a prize to the team that gets the most signatures within the given time frame. Some ideas for categories are:

1. Someone who has dyed her hair a different color
2. Someone who was born in the same month as someone in the youth group
3. Someone whose last name begins with the same letter as someone's in the youth group
4. Someone who has been to Hawaii on vacation
5. Someone who drives a convertible

Variation: Instead of going out into the neighborhood searching for people to sign the category lists, play this game with your own youth in the cultural hall of your ward meetinghouse. Each youth should have a category list and a pencil and must obtain signatures from other players who fit the categories on his list.

Silly Fashion Show

To begin this activity, explain to the youth that they are going to be "models" in a silly fashion show. For the first part of the activity, they should design their costumes, and for the second part of the activity they will perform the fashion show on the stage of your cultural hall. Costumes for the fashion show must include play-on words such as:

1. Bear-back gown (teddy bear strapped to one's back)
2. Pin-stripe pants (safety pins pinned vertically in stripes down one's pants)
3. Plunging neck-line (toilet plunger tied around one's neck)
4. Bell-bottom pants (jingle bells fastened to the ankles of one's pant legs)
5. Dress with capped sleeves (baseball caps fastened to shoulders of dress)

Either let the youth come up with their own costume ideas or give them a list of suggestions. Assign a youth leader to act as the announcer. He should use a microphone to tell the audience about each outfit as someone models it. Consider video taping this performance so that the youth can watch themselves on television for a good laugh later!

Square Dancing

Arrange to have a good square dance caller offer his services at this activity. Tell the youth to dress in Western attire, and learn how to square dance together by following instructions from the caller. This activity might be especially authentic if it is held outdoors or in a barn.

Thirties Dinner

Advertise this combined activity as a "Thirties Dinner." Encourage the youth to come dressed like they were from the 1930's era. When they get to the activity, have a soup line set up for them featuring soups and breads, resembling the Depression. As the youth eat, let a speaker give a presentation to the youth about life during the Depression and the importance of cultivating gratitude for the abundance of blessings we enjoy today.

Three Legged Sports Night

Divide your group of youth into pairs. Have the pairs stand side by side while you tie their inside legs together. Then, while the pairs remain tied together, play several sports such as soccer, basketball, volleyball, and softball.

Toe Races

For this activity, divide the youth into teams of 4-5 people each. Give each team about 30 small objects that can be carried with one's toes, such as a marble, a pencil, and a penny. Each team should have the same types of objects. Instruct all team members to take their shoes and socks off of their feet and stand in line, one behind the other, at a starting line. Place a bucket for each team at a finish line about 15 feet away from where they are standing. Teams should spread out their objects near them at the starting line. At the "go" signal, one person from each team races to pick up one object using only his toes, carry it down to the bucket, and deposit the object into the bucket. He then runs back to the starting line, tags the next team member, and goes to the back of the line. When tagged, the second team member picks up another object with her toes, carries it to the bucket, drops it inside, and runs back to tag the third member of the team. Play continues in this fashion until one team successfully drops all 30 of its objects into its bucket, thus winning the game.

Trivia Scavenger Hunt

Divide the youth into teams of about four people each, and give each team a list of trivia questions and a pencil. Teams must go from house to house searching for people who can give them the correct answers to the trivia questions on their lists. The teams can get only one answer per household and must return to the ward building at a designated time, finished or not. After the teams return to the church, announce the correct answers to the trivia questions. Award a prize to the team that collected the most correct answers. Some examples of trivia questions are:

1. What do you call a baby kangaroo?
2. In what country would you find the "Blarney Stone"?
3. In the movie The Princess Bride, what does Wesley say while rolling down the hill?
4. In what year did Disneyland open?
5. What type of sea creature stuns its prey by using sound waves before eating it?

Variation: Instead of asking trivia questions from a wide variety of topics, focus on questions of a single topic such as "animals," "world geography," "religion," "music groups," "automobiles," or "movies."

Variety Show

Host a ward youth variety show in which each of the young men and young women must perform an act on stage for the others. The acts can be silly skits, comedy routines, or talent displays. If you turn this activity into a talent show, remember that all talents are not in the visual arts and encourage those with talents in other areas besides the visual arts to display, read, or explain their talents rather than just perform on stage.

**May help fulfill a Mia Maid 1 Individual Worth Value Experience and a Mia Maid 2 Knowledge Value Experience*

Video Scavenger Hunt

Divide the youth into teams of about four people each, and give each team a list of things to film on video during a certain time period (about 45 minutes). At the "go" signal, teams should leave the ward meetinghouse and go around the neighborhood, video taping the things on their lists. After time is up, all teams return back to the church and watch the videos they have made. Some things teams might video:

1. A police siren blaring
2. A stoplight turning yellow
3. A cow mooing
4. A baby with a pacifier in its mouth
5. Someone getting a strike at a bowling alley

Water Brigade

For this water game, split your youth into two groups. On each team, one guy sits cross legged on the grass with a bucket between his legs, holding a cup on his head. A blindfolded girl scoops water out of a pail and walks toward him. The only person who can give her directions as to where to walk is one of her teammates who is holding a mirror in his hand with his back toward her. He looks in the mirror and tries to direct her to the guy with the cup on his head and then gives her directions as to how to pour the water into the cup. When her cup is empty, the guy dumps his cup into the bucket between his legs. The girl pulls her blindfold off and runs it to the person with the mirror who puts the blindfold on and repeats the procedure. The next teammate in line takes the mirror and directs him with it. Time this water game to see which team can get the most water in its bucket in a given amount of time.

Water Relays

On a large grassy field, provide several different water relay races for the youth. For all of the relays listed, divide your group of youth into teams of about eight people per team. Give each team a bucket of water at the starting line and an empty bucket at a finish line across the field. For all relays, the object of the game is for a team to end up with the most water in its bucket at the finish line when a given time limit expires. The rules for the relays vary as follows:

1. Sponge Relay: Soak a sponge and toss it across the field to a person waiting to receive it. He catches it and squeezes the water into an empty bucket before tossing it back for the next player to soak and throw.
2. Water Balloon Throw: Each team member takes turns tossing a water balloon across the field to a person who catches it and breaks it into the bucket.
3. Balance The Teaspoon: One team member carries water in a teaspoon across the field and dumps it into the bucket. She then runs back to the starting line and gives the teaspoon to the next team member.
4. Hand Ladle: A team member carries water in his cupped hands across the field and empties it into an empty bucket. He then races back to the starting line and tags the next team member so he can follow suit.
5. Hair Wringing: One team member dumps her hair into a full bucket of water, runs across the field, and wrings it out into the empty bucket. She then races back to the starting line and tags the next team mem-

ber so he can follow suit. (A towel can be used instead of hair for this relay.)

Wheelbarrow Water Race

Divide the youth into teams of 2-4 people each. Prepare a wheelbarrow obstacle course. The course is to be run by one or two teammates pushing the wheelbarrow with the other one or two people inside the wheelbarrow along with a five-gallon bucket full of water. Each team must get its wheelbarrow to the end of the obstacle course in the fastest time possible with the most water left in the bucket. Some ideas of obstacles over which each wheelbarrow must pass: in and out of a line of orange construction cones, over a dirt hill, through a puddle of water, along a straight line or sidewalk curb, over a bridge or ramp, or over a bed of rocks.

Index